Pieces of Myself
Based on True Poetry

Table of Contents

PART I
PIECES OF MY SOUL

Chapter 1 My Mother and Me

Just Listen

Ma

What Did She Do?

The Main Things I want to Know

Baby, That Was Jesus

Way More than You Could Ever Imagine

Even When It Hurts

As If It All Never Happened

Chapter 2 My Father and Me

My Point of View

I Don't Remember You

Free From the Tree

D.A.N

<u>Chapter 3 My Adorable three and Me</u>

A Message to My Kids

I'm Daddy

The Apple That Fell Far from The Tree

Julicia Regina Neshea Clemons

Jutaurio P. Clemons Jr.

Ju'niyah Yashea Clemons

She Told Me She Loves Him

Boogey Man

To My Jr.

With All My Breath

Love Flower

Daddy's Love

To Fly a Kite

<u>Chapter 4 Others and Me</u>

Lil Tyree

You Almost Messed Up

Physical Education

Passive and Aggressive

A Letter to My Homie

Jay-Z

Marlene's Mother

My Auntie... Your Still My Mother

Memories of An Old Friend

Bite the Lemon

Invisible Tears

More Than Me

I Really Do Love You

Paulonda

A Mother-in-Law

Love from the Core

My Appreciation

Carlos

T.J.M.S

Spoken Words

PART II

PIECES OF MY HEART

Chapter 5 Her & Me

A Poem from Her

The 3 of Us

A Note to My Love

Only You Can Make Me Happy

I Regret

Where is Yesterday

A Flower

I Need You

Hearts

Birthdays

At Times Love Is

If Love Was…

Why Didn't You Just Stay?

Broken Hearts

Say What You Need to Say

Mr. Emotional

How To Love

The Girl Who Changed My Heart

Happy Mother's Day

Thinking About You

Chapter 6: My thoughts and Me

It's All Over

Against All Odds

I'm Aware You Think I'm Not

That's Just My Baby Momma

Crack

A Man's Life and Chess

Doing My Best

Keep Trying

Me, Myself, and I

My Generation

I'm Just Living

Define Women

Get Away

Do They Really Feel Me?

I Wonder What He Wonders

All That's Shown

Time

Lady Justice

Chapter 7: My Feelings and Me

The Wickedness That Lies

Questions

It's Been Written

My Fire

I Didn't Die

Understand Me

Written With Tears

Cry

Because of You

If I Die Before I Wake

Chapter 8: My Pen and Me

Breathe-Write

With This Pen

I'm A Writer

The Caged Bird That Wrote

I Just Write

I'd Rather Be a Writer

What I Write

What I Write Now

What I Continue to Write

Before I'm Told I Can't Write

More Than Just Writing

Introduction

Since I was a young boy, I've always enjoyed writing. I would pour out my thoughts and feelings on paper. I was an outcast so I kind of became my own best friend. I was literate at a very young age, due to my mother being serious about education. She would provide us, my two younger brothers and I with all kinds of books. As a child, books gave me a creative imagination, and the more I would read, the more I would write. At first, I found it difficult to write stories, so I wrote poetry, and then a story was told. I learned that writing is healthy for my soul. So, every chance I got I would write my reaction to whatever action or thought at hand. Through my writing I could be me, I could get away from the world surrounding me. I could cry without being criticized about," how men aren't supposed to cry." I could smile through written words. I feel how I feel so that's what I write. I write to leave behind all of who I am. So, I write to guide, to understand, and to make a difference. As I write, there's something at that very moment that inspires me to write. I don't just write and make things up. What I write is created from emotions, thoughts, and actions. It is a part of me, the things that I write I give it life when I write. I learned that we must fit into our own lives, instead of always trying to fit into others' lives where we fit in. I can't recall me fitting in ever. No one understood me, although they'd understand what I write. When I write they know how I feel, what I think, what I believe, my understanding, my fears, my tears, and my dreams all because of what I write. One day my thoughts and feelings will come to an end, but the things that I write will be read forever.

PART I

PIECES OF MY SOUL

Chapter 1: My mother and me

"...By sorrow of the heart the spirit is broken."
-Proverbs 15:13

Just Listen

Understand who I am based on where I've been, to bring me where I am. That will lead me to where I'm going.
Pain keeps me going and love has become so foreign. Blood will shed like all my tears to endure no more fears.
I'd rather staple my eyelids then to be forced to witness the pain that comes from my kids.
I've loved and I've hated; about killing myself I've contemplated. Over and over, with myself, I've debated.
I've always felt I had God's protection; still I was lost without direction.
Be aware of the change in due time. So, I'll be patient to get what's mine, even if it takes dying. But no more lying, crying, or calling myself trying. I'll just do what I've got to do; always to myself I'll be true. I've got to be me,
I can't be you. Things happened that you never knew. Not once have you ever asked me what I've been through.
You witnessed me as a boy, become stranger and stranger. You didn't realize I was sick with so much anger. Walking with less instruction caused self-destruction. Much frustration caused me to lose my concentration.
I heard things, I observe things, I did things it hurts to say. I tried to show you in my own way, the pain caused my childhood to go astray.
There's so much you were missing and all I ever wanted was for you to just listen.

Inspired by my mother, the lack of communication, love, pain, and a big misunderstanding.

Dedicated to my mother Regina.

Ma

Biggest fear was having to identify your first born dead.
Still, I was your baby boy with a hard head.
Being the oldest had my heart the coldest.
You always did your best, even when you ended up with
less; kept a smile under all the stress.
I was lost and didn't want to be found.
Although I shamed you, still you would come around.
There was a lot within I knew I could achieve,
it hurt me at times when you didn't believe.
I just knew things would get better as long as I pray.
I wonder do you miss me as a boy, yellin" Ma!" all day.

Inspired by thoughts of my childhood mother.

Dedicated to my mother, July 14, 2008.

<u>What Did She Do?</u>

I look at him and ask myself, "What did she do?"

"Why he hitten 'my momma?" I said.

"Why he hitten 'my momma?" he said.

"What's wrong momma?" I said.

"What's wrong momma?" he said.

"Why you crying momma?" I said.

"Why you crying momma?" he said.

I'm watching a man beat my momma.

He's watching me beat his momma.

I see me, while I'm looking at him; I wonder if he's asking himself, what did she do?

Inspired by love, pain, experience, guilt, shame, observation, and being observed.

Dedicated to my mother, my sons' mother, and to the little boy who watched and became. 2008.

The Main Things I want to Know

If you hurt, why do you smile?

If you want to cry, why do you laugh?

If you're tired, why do you continue to stay?

If you don't want to, why do you anyway?

I know you're the mother and I'm the son. With the many questions I want to ask, these are the main things I want to know.

Inspired by unanswered questions.

Dedicated to my mother and passiveness. May 03, 2011.

Baby, That Was Jesus

I remember a homeless man was walking by on a hot summer's day.
A breeze came through as all the children play.
This man asked my mother for some food,
because he was hungry.
His clothes were dirty, and his hair was dingy.
She quickly went to the kitchen and prepared a dish of oodles and noodles. She gave him a recycled butter bowl full of food. I wanted to interrupt, but I knew I couldn't be rude.
I watched him accept the food and walk away.
I looked up at my mother curiously, and said,
"Ma, why did you give that man our food?"
She put her hand on my shoulder, smiled, and said
"Baby, that was Jesus,".

Inspired by love, understanding, and many blessings to come.

Dedicated to my mother, a sweet woman, May 5, 2011.

Way More Than You Could Ever Imagine

If I could make you happy I would,
just to be a part of something that makes you feel good.
If you'd tell me your darkest secrets I'd sit and listen.
If I could complete you, I'd be all that's missing.
To prove my love, for you I'd kill.
Then in blood our bond will be sealed.
I don't think you utterly understand how I feel.
I love you with a profound intimacy, yet it's not sexual.
You didn't try hard enough to save your first born.
I didn't understand how one day my entire life became torn.
I wonder why you don't mention my spirit being crushed.
Inside of me is that 12-year-old boy who misses his mother so much.
I love you with every beat of my heart.
Never should we have been apart.
There're so many things that are left unsaid.
So, I write hoping what I write don't go unread.
I want to give you smiles so I can make up
for the tears that you've shed.
Regardless of all that has happened,
still, I love you way more than you could ever imagine.

Inspired by love, hate, a bond, a first-born love for his mother, and things kept in the dark.

Dedicated it to my mother. June 4th, 2011

Even When It Hurts

It was me, Shea, and Shaad. She gave birth to Four sons, still she didn't understand the love of God.
Some say children are His gifts. For every wildflower, there's a smile; and for every raindrop, there's a tear.
As the moon glows and reflect off the sea, there's someone, somewhere they don't want to be.
Some say the best things in life are free. Or is it just being free the best thing in life? Since day one, no one quite understood me. Yet you were also unaware of who I'd be.
As I lived, witnessed, and endured, I knew you were all I had; but with having you, I assumed things wouldn't have been so bad.
I felt like I was nothing, so all I wanted was just a piece of something.
I didn't have anything, so I went after everything.
Tears are bitter, and like lemons; they can be made sweet.
"Ma, I needed you. I really didn't like the streets!"
I remember the days you'd go without new clothes just so your boys could have new shirts, that's why I love you even when it hurts.

Inspired by a love-hate relationship.

Dedicated to my mother, August 13th, 2011.

As If It All Never Happened

Everyone told you to put your husband before your first born. When he came along that's when all the madness began.
You act like nothing was done.
You constantly had me arrested, not knowing that every time
I was constantly being neglected.
You even got on the stand and all I could think about was the love you had for this man.
You wouldn't't allow me, your flesh and blood, in your home. That's when all my innocence was gone.
Everywhere I went I would hear "poor thing,"
a song your old neighborhood friends would sing.
You'd smile in my face even held me in a tight embrace and whispered that you love me.
You told me it was tough love; that's like spitting in my face.
Like a husband who kicks his wife, saying he does it "out of love." That's one hell of a kick, but what you did was more than just sick.
It was detrimental to my soul; the only reason my heart turned cold. Since I was able to open my eyes before I knew the truth in lies.
I wanted you to see me, your boy, be the best that I could be. We were supposed to be a team, and together chase our dreams; I guess you got tired of chasing them way before I got on the scene.
Despite it all my love for you, you wouldn't imagine.
Still, you go on as if it all never happened.

Inspired by all that did happen.

Dedicated to my mother, June 13th, 2011.

Chapter 2: My Fathers & Me

"Fathers, do not provoke your children lest they become discouraged."

-Colossians 3:21

My Point of View

I try hard to find myself, yet it's like the harder I try the more I seem to lose myself.

I'm in a state of mind where everything around me is an illusion and so much confusion.

I try to block it out; most of the time I cry and shout.

I'm inviting you to look at life through my eyes. What you are seeing, it's not a nightmare; it's my perception of the world.

My body don't need warmth, but my cold heart alone.

Sadness and sorrows bring pain, which creates an agonizing hatred towards others.

You'll probably never feel how I feel,

and if you do, you'll know life isn't a thrill.

Your smiles and laughter are all so touching.

Behind my smile is pain and suffering. My happy thoughts are of a joyful 14-year-old boy playing with his father.

Instead of cursing and fighting when his son does something wrong, he corrects him in a firm yet motivating tone.

Now back to reality where my dad is out smoking crack and I'm 14-years-old looking for a purse to snatch.

Looking in the mirror, seeing his reflection, and hating it.

Making sure my daughter and I have a father-daughter connection.

If I could ask one question it would be "why?"

Deep down in the depths of my heart I wish he would die.

All my agony is because of you. Now I know the meaning of a good father: that's the total opposite of you.

Only if you knew what you've created.

And no one wants to look at it from my point of view.

Inspired by pain and being fatherless.

Dedicated it to my biological father, 2003.

I Don't Remember You

I remember the first man I called, "Dad." I don't
remember it being you.
I remember the crowd going wild when I hit my first home
run. I don't remember you being in the bleachers.
I remember talking to my first girlfriend. I don't remember
talking to you about her. I remember having my first child,
hearing her say granddaddy for the first time. I don't
remember it being you she looked at. Growing through
life I remember I was down and out. I don't remember
you being there. Now at 22 years of age, I sit and
remember everything in my life. But I don't remember
you.

Inspired by pain, growth, experience, and not being able
to remember.

Dedicated to my biological father. June 11, 2008.

Free From the Tree

You didn't fail as a father because you didn't even try.
I was just a boy when I used to ask "why?" Now I write
just to feel like I can fly. I'm nothing like you and I look
just like you. I remember when I first became a father.
It was 12 years ago this exact day. I knew I would love
her in the best way. It hurts me that I'm not around. But
your presence I never found. I used to dream about you
just giving it a try. Then in my dreams you would die. But
the strange thing is, I'd cry. **For you I've shed tears and
been embarrassed in the presence of my peers.** She
didn't want you, so you didn't want me. Despite being in
prison, I'm free. Free from the tree.

Inspired by being a father, and my father who didn't even
try.

Dedicated to my biological father. October 27, 2013.

D.A.N

I had many names because I tried to change the picture; still, the frame remained the same. I was eager to be accepted wherever I went, so I began to camouflage my surroundings and my time spent. I was just a kid trying to fit in. You should've let me be a child and allow time to take its course. Instead, you cheated me out of my childhood without any remorse. You accused me of this just because you assumed that. You were the first man who I witnessed abuse alcohol, used drugs, and curse at my mother. To be honest you were worse than any other. How could you be so quick to judge and after all these years, continue to hold a grudge? I was a boy in desperate need of a father to be true. I didn't deserve the things you put me through, or to be accused of the things that I didn't do. I didn't have anyone this you knew, but you still took my mother away. At the tender age of thirteen, in your home I couldn't stay. For you I would even pray that God allow you to understand me one day. I was 12 years old; I needed a helping hand, not to be called D.A.N. Rather, encourage me to do the best that I can. You chose to suppress how you felt and call me, just a boy, D.A.N.

Inspired by hate, cold nights, a lost childhood, misunderstanding, and all the things I didn't do to be called D.A.N (Dumb Ass Nigga)

Dedicated to a stepfather, June 03, 2011

Chapter 3: My adorable Three & Me

"Children are a heritage from the lord."
-Psalms 127:3

A message to My kids

Stay away from dope and guns. Seek knowledge and understanding,
a message to my son. Keep your head up and reach for the stars.
Stay positive and I promise you'll dodge these bars.
Yes, you're gorgeous, stay pure like water. Daddy loves you all, a message to my daughters. I know life isn't easy so just do your best. I promise the three of you. God will do the rest. Go all the way with your education. You'll need it in this world you're facing. My freedom I've been deprived. That's why I've been absent in all your lives.
I can't change all the things I did, but before I die, I can leave a message to my kids.

Inspired by experience, love, maturity and being a father.

Dedicated to my children; Julicia, Jutaurio Jr, and Ju'niyah. 2008.

I'm Daddy

I know you can't see me, yet I'm still there.
I'm your favorite food,
I'm your favorite pair of shoes.
I'm your favorite cartoon.
I'm your favorite song.
I'm what makes you laugh and smile,
and I'm your blood that flows through you.
I'm the reflection you see in the mirror.
I'm Daddy.

Inspired by being absent in their lives.

Dedicated to my children whom I adore and love. 2008.

The Apple That Fell Far from The Tree

They say he looks just like me,
he has my ways, still his future we'll have to wait and see.
I know within he'll fall far away from this tree. He'll take a
different path to be all he can be.
I was one of those apples that didn't get too far. Still, I strive to
show my own the way. Also, to discuss things my parents
never got the chance to say. Some things are hereditary. Most
things we do as parents aren't necessary. For our young we all
want what's best for them to become extraordinary, much
different from the rest.
I sit back while contemplating deep thoughts about teaching
my son to be a man something I wasn't taught.
Strive for excellence and wait for what's to come.
All trees aren't good, yet there are some.
Although, I look like the eldest tree
and the apple looks like me,
there so much more about
the apple that fell far away from the tree.

Inspired by wanting more for my son, and those who
overcome the cycle.

Dedicated to My Jr., and all those who became more than the
tree. May 07, 2011.

J.R.N.C

I remember when your mother was pregnant.
I couldn't wait to meet you, contemplating on all the things I'd
teach you.
You're my first born, my oldest girl, the first one I created
into this world. At school all the other fathers were there.
I know you felt that it wasn't fair.
I love you so much and I want you to be all you can be.
I want you to be better than your mother and me.
I need you to take care of your siblings if something ever goes
wrong.
In your heart they should always have a home.
I thank your mother for doing her best.
She kept you straight. I'm a man now and daddy's here,
so, in this world there's nothing to fear.
Daddy made a lot of mistakes but being away from you again
is one I refuse to make.
Put a smile on your face, you don't have to frown.
I promise you that I won't let you down.

Inspired by love, absence, maturity, and being a father.

Dedicated to my Princess Juju. July 12th, 2008.

Jutaurio Jr.

Lil Ju, I'm sorry. There are things I should've done that I didn't do. Overall, your daddy loves you. You're my only boy; you even have my name. You're my pride and joy. I want you to know and understand. I was doing all I can. Now Daddy's a better man. I need you to grow into a decent young man. Give your mother keys to her own land. I often ponder in life who you'll be. Son, know that in this world nothing is free. Yet anything in this world is earned through hard work. Since you were born, I told myself I'll give you a pen, paper, and a thousand books, before I allow you to run with crooks. Read all that I write to know what it took. Son, you can trust and believe me; I'll be there. Although there's things I didn't get done, always know that I love you, son.

Inspired by love, absence, maturity and being a father.

Dedicated to the Prince. July 12, 2008.

J.Y.C

A.K.A. Ms. Pretty, my Niyah. With your smile, nothing could get me higher. You're my little princess and I love you like I love the rest. I'm sorry that as a newborn I couldn't hold you to my chest.
I am locked down, that's why Daddy isn't around. As the months and years come to pass. I watch you grow through pictures that seldom come. With whatever you hear about your father, know that I love you. I missed you as a baby, still I'll raise you to be a young lady.

Inspired by love, absence, maturity, and being a father.

Dedicated to my Dooka. I love you. July 12th, 2008.

She Told Me She Loved Him

I was dumbfounded when she told me,
I couldn't believe my ears.
That was one of my biggest fears.
She told me he makes her laugh and hold her when she
cries. She goes on and on; I sit and continue to listen,
knowing these are valuable times I'm missing.
I'm a man so what she feels I understand.
I wish I were the one she loved,
but how so, when right now,
at this very moment I can't even give her a hug.
Of course, it makes me sad thinking of the things with her
I never had.
Because she's my daughter and I'm her real Dad.

Inspired by a visit from my baby daughter, telling me that
she loves her stepfather. Despite that, I'm glad she's
happy.

Dedicated to my daughter and her stepdad

Boogey Man

Why would you do that? What is wrong with you? She was only seven years old. You would still be doing it if she never would've told. You thought she liked it. She's curious to the world. That's because she was seven; she was just a little girl. They act as if you did nothing wrong. God knows what I would've done if I were home. I feel at times it's my fault. I just thank God you got caught. Who knew the things you did to deprive her of her innocence? Only she knows what really went on, the feelings aren't shown and probably will go unknown. She smiles to hide the pain. Still, she shed tears when memories fill her brain. You can't imagine what you've done. The rapture isn't over; it's just begun. Eventually a lot of little girls would run and hide. I never would've thought one of them would've been mine. Somebody should've seen a sign. Some will say she's lying and go on as if they're blind. A part of her in the inside has run away and died. No one will ever understand her tears…unless they've been touched by the Boogey Man.

Inspired by my daughter's tears.

Dedicated to Julicia. I'm so sorry I wasn't there. I love you. June 16th, 2009.

<u>To My Jr.</u>

A cloud of smoke can't produce fire, and a puddle of water can't make rain.
Trying to make someone love you is quite the same.
Wisdom isn't knowledge and all fluids can't be made solid. We're all considered men despite now or then.
I think what makes us the same is where we've been.
People believe with their hearts what they can't see.
But what their eyes witness, they'll disagree.
Now if that makes our minds imprisoned, how will we ever be free? Now I don't know about you, but I know about me.
I know I love what love could be.
I know I'll eventually make a way,
and I thank God for you being born seven years ago on this day.

Inspired by thoughts of everything seen and done and a message to my boy.

Dedicated to Jutaurio Jr, The Prince. July 19th, 2011.

<u>With All My Breath</u>

Your heart is the reflection of my soul.
Your actions are in accord with your mother's teachings.
You'll be the woman you want to be,
yet I know you'll copy what your eyes see.
I'm not there to guide you to stand on values.
So now you're not stationed like a boat without anchor.
I try to be more conscious and a thinker.
I love you more than written or spoken words would ever
say. Respect yourself, understand yourself, and most of
all believe in yourself. Nobody will love you like you love
yourself. Remember always, Daddy loves you with all my
breath.

Inspired by observing my daughter's ways.

Dedicated to Princess Juju. 2012.

Love Flower

Do you mind if I tell you a story?
No matter fiction or none. Some won't understand,
some will take in all that was done.
He was young, she was younger.
Deep inside, her pain I often ponder.
Embracing love somehow, we often wonder.
It's been a while like five summers.
She smiled for me when inside she had been hurting.
All because a Boogey Man had been lurking.
I wasn't there, it wasn't fair.
Do that to my love child, how could you dare?
Seeds were planted and thoughts grew.
He's a product of his household, some escape, but just a
few. I found out late, I was so hurt inside.
I can't believe some say she lied.
I be high on pain, but her smiles make me sober.
I'm out of touch, yet I'm tuned in.
I'm so far away, and every day for her I pray.
Things are getting better,
and I tell her birds of a feather flock together.
So now she changes clothes and hide her toes.
 Deep inside how she feels no one really knows.
We made a promise to each other to forever be honest.
And her being a lady consist of her being modest.
So, the story end…No not ever we just keep on going.
So, the love can keep growing.
Don't worry about those who hurt you let it go,
because I promise you, they'll reap what they sow.
For now, forgive and watch the love flower grow.

Inspired by my daughter's smile that dried her tears.

Dedicated to Julicia. January 7th, 2013.

Daddy's Love

When I think of you, I see rainbows and deep rivers of
honey flow. The love I have for you inside you must
know. Your smile is radiant, a bright glow.
I think of you all the time.
Knowing there isn't a daughter as sweet as mine.
When the sun dries all the rain, understand that's a sign.
That one day we'll all stop crying.
I love you with my soul and all that's in me.
I promise you there's no place I'd rather be.
Then with all my children home free.
You're getting older, and it'll make you so much bolder.
But always remember as long as you have self-respect.
There won't be much you regret.
If I could just give you one big hug,
you'd feel all your daddy's love.

Inspired by time and love.

Dedicated to Julicia. May 25th, 2014.

<u>To Fly a Kite</u>

I wish I could show you how to fly a kite.
To allow you to enjoy keeping your head up to the sky.
And when the weather's bad, you'll have memories that
drives your hopes for tomorrow.
That one day you'll lift your head high in the sky
while enjoying the kite you fly.

Inspired by missing out on so much and talking to my
daughter.

Dedicated to Julicia, November 22nd, 2017.

Chapter 4: Others & Me

"The righteous should choose his friends carefully, for the way of the wicked leads them astray."

-Proverbs 12:26

Lil Tyree

So talented and so determined to be great.
Your mother did all she could do to keep you straight,
she kept things together when it got rough on her plate.
We never know our future and God chooses our fate,
not realizing it's the life choices we make.
I didn't know you as a young man,
but me being me, I understand that wasn't part of the
plan.
I know your mother did all she can,
and she'll always be your number one fan.
Although I'm older we shared a childhood.
Back then it was all good,
it wasn't about different faces or going to unusual places.
It was about hitting homeruns and stealing bases.
We were friends, close like next of kin.
Know we will love you until the end, until we meet again.

Inspired by friendship and sudden absence.

Dedicated to Tyree in the event of his demise.
December 23rd, 2008.

You Almost Messed Up

You made it twelve hard years…

You almost messed up.

I'm so proud of you for making it out…

You almost messed up.

I'm so glad you didn't end up like me…

You almost messed up.

Just thinking how life would be if you wouldn't have
almost messed up, but you did? When things get rough
at times, and you want to give up.
You've got to remember when you almost messed up.

Inspired by brotherly love, patience, April 10th, 2007, and
overcoming adversities.

Dedicated to my brother Erik Fennell, June 15th, 2008.

Physical Education

More than a P.E. teacher,
she's a blessing to those who meet her.
 A woman with beauty deeper than her features.
I was young, chasing the wind,
not able to understand the true essence of a friend.
She was strong and didn't let her morals bend.
I didn't get why she gave me a book.
She was encouraging me to read.
So, to win I knew what it took.
I wish somehow, she knew,
after all these years I finally grew.
Wherever she is in this world I'd sail.
Just to let her know I didn't fail.
That I finally got the message she wanted me to receive.
When it hit me I fell down to my knees.
She let me know the sky was mine to achieve.
I wish I could have just one more conversation with the
angel I met in Physical Education.

Inspired by a P.E. teacher who encouraged me to never
give up and be all I can be. She gave me a book, 'Gifted
Hands,' signed by Dr. Ben Carson.

Dedicated to Mrs. Young. 2009.

Passive & Aggressive

Both beautiful with radiant smiles,
yet one endures a massive amount of pain.
One has many friends, the other barely has any at all.
One is selfish while the other is always there when you
call.
It's not about being selfish, more of self-preservation.
As far as the other, she'll help you so much to the point of
losing her own observation. One understands self while
the other is in search of self.
One won't go for anything, while with the other, anything
goes.
I understand one since the other is understanding.
I believe in them both, yet they both don't believe.
One, he didn't bother, the other didn't understand the
love of a father.
One can't give birth as far as the other I am her first.
One agrees while the other disagree, they love each
other unconditionally.
One's an aunt and one's a mother.
They allowed life to take its course,
their hearts together create a phenomenal force.
I look deep within her eyes
and hold her close to see within what lies.
One I love while the other holds my heart.
Passive & Aggressive are so close apart.
Inspired by love, understanding, sisterhood,
misunderstanding and being a son to two sisters.

Dedicated to my mother and auntie (Cheena & Pookie).

A Letter to My Homie

Jason, wuz up, how's things on the other side?
Last time we talked I felt bad; that's why I cried.
I tried to keep my head up and keep it real.
But the ones I would've died for can't imagine how I feel.
It's been a while since I saw your daughter, Tynesha, holding
her down, keeping her in order. She's just like you, I swear
she's something else.
I feel I let you down; still, I feel you understand.
I was just a boy transforming into a man.
I hate that you left without me.
It should've been someone else whose soul was set free.
Ms. Brenda still wilding and I love her to death.
Pooh Bear still thuggin,' taking care of himself.
Teara…haven't heard from her in a while.
Leola is a woman now; she even got a child.
I miss you, homie, from the heart.
You dying, I didn't get that part.
I was just checkin' in until we meet
so, hold it down up there and keep me a seat.

P.S. Tell God I'm trying my best and I'm sorry I didn't pass the
test.
Inspired by missing my homie. Dedicated to Jason
Underwood, 2009.

Jay-Z

You're someone I always admired.
My father...who? Nah...nah...I'm the boy Jay-z.
You taught me too just be all I can be.
Now that's the true meaning of a real 'G.'
Even if the majority disagree,
because I hold the key to my own destiny.
I'm locked down, still I'm free.
This is what I'm all about,
without contradiction or a reasonable doubt.
The obstacles I come upon I'll just brush my shoulders off,
win some and take some as a loss.
I'm giving it all I've got; how can I fail?
No matter this cell or any jail.
You've got a queen and that's a blessing God brings.
She was your Bonnie first, then she told you to put a ring on it.
Blueprint one and two guided me through.
Taught me to stay smooth on my feet.
I close my eyes and listen to you recite over the beat.
I couldn't let them fall down my eyes,
so, I felt relieved when you made the song cry.
Then I realized I got ninety-nine problems and she ain't one;
the track goes on and on and we rock the next song.
Yet every time I think you're gone.
you drop again and have my mind blown.
Keep doing you because I'm going to keep doing me.
That's what I learned from the boy Jay-Z.
Inspired by listening and learning.

Dedicated to Shawn Carter. June 6th, 2009.

Marlene's Mother

I remember when you allowed me in your home when I had nowhere else to go.
The Spirit of God within you would glow,
and in the midst of the storm, it would show.
I'm ashamed about the time I was in your presence and didn't acknowledge you.
Who I was, I knew you knew.
It was jealousy of a woman that made me do what I did.
I think of you often,
praying that I get a chance to apologize before I lay in a coffin.
Your daughter held a piece of my heart.
I wasn't prepared to be a man.
it was best that she departs, because I was wrong from the start.
Well, this isn't about her, but you. So, I want to thank you for the smiles and the understanding.

Inspired by a beautiful soul and a God-fearing woman.

Dedicated to Marlene's mother. 2010.

My Auntie…Still You're My Mother

You're my Auntie, yet so much more like my mother.
You've given me all I need, although I wasn't your seed.
I love you with more than my heart alone.
I don't know what I'll do without you in my life.
I admire your style and grace.
Yes, you're the sister of my mother, but you're a part of me like no other.
We live and we learn, and as far as mistakes, we'll all have our turn.
I am the son you never had.
My soul was birthed through another, yet you're still my mother.

Inspired by triumphs, shortcomings, a nephew, an aunt, a son, and a mother.

Dedicated to Carla Mornings (I love you Pookie). May 2nd, 2011.

Memories of an Old Friend

Masculine in personality, yet so feminine in her
demeanor.
Beautiful within and so different from the average.
Secrets of love and fidelity she conceals.
A mother that holds a deep sex appeal.
She smiles in the light, still she shed tears in the dark.
She dreams of awakening in a universe far away from
Central Park.
Lost her first love to death, holding on to memories of his
last breath.
Was an outcast, still she fit in.
Her smile is radiant as well as her tears are piercing to
the heart.
Her soul is strong, yet her heart is weak.
A woman you would love to meet.
Quiet like the sky before a storm,
still strong like the ocean that holds up battleships.
Eyes graceful with soft, full lips.
She's stylish with her own trend.
Just a few memories of an old friend.

Inspired by my best friend coming up.

Dedicated to Anquetta M. (I miss you from the heart.)
May 9th, 2011.

Bite the Lemon

Something once sour, now so sweet.
Was lost but stands on her own two feet.
It's ironic how a flower grows in a storm.
The worst weather, imagine a young woman in a snowstorm.
Without the slightest comfort of a sweater,
but she holds on and even smiles when it hurts
Because despite her actions, she knows better.
That she should put her kids first.
Things may seem sweet but end up sour.
So, we go back to the kodak of the young woman and the flower.
Ran to the streets and got accustomed to misfortunes.
Without ever taking time out for what's important,
finally realizing adversities will come and we'll all have our portion.
We've shared tears away from our peers.
When my heart was broken and couldn't seem to heal,
she said, "keep your head up, let her go, I know how you feel."
I didn't quite understand that she could see within my strengths as a man.
I can remember one night we shared dinner amongst friends:
A fancy restaurant, a different kind of blend.
We had our own team who started trends.
I'd sit back and we were laughing right away, not worried about the past or future, just focused on that day.
Not really focused on how life can be sour.
So, you live life and make each day count, and when you add it all up, you'll get a good amount. Remember me, who told you to "bite the lemon."

Inspired by friendship, love, observation, and memories.

Dedicated to @columbian_mina, 2011.

<u>Invisible Tears</u>

A beautiful girl forced to be a woman, who smiles to hide her pain.
An angel trapped in hell with nowhere to turn.
The world is so cold, the hard way she had to learn.
Experienced so much she's moved by the slightest touch.
Been beaten and abused.
It's like she couldn't win even if everyone else would lose.
Ran to drugs to make up for the lack of hugs.
I remember nights we'd talk and open our hearts.
She'd tell me I didn't belong here because I was way too smart.
I'd sit and wonder how life could go so wrong from the start.
When she gave birth to her first born,
she knew what it took to be a good mother.
I don't know if I ever told her, but I loved you like a brother.
I always saw something special inside of you.
Forget about the rest, just do your best.
You have characteristics more attractive and real,
more unique than any sex appeal.
Although time has come and gone, and love may go unshown,
hold your head up and face your fears.
Dry your eyes and wipe away your invisible tears.
Inspired by observation, understanding and friendship.

Dedicated to Latoya June 5th, 2011.

More Than Me

Being that I was confused about my sexuality and didn't quite understand,
I decided to hide behind being a ladies' man.
When it came to sports and education, I'd practice until tears or blood was shed, when no one else knew.
Just to be told I was better for doing what others couldn't do.
I was scared so I chased him, to run from them.
I cheated if I felt I'd be defeated.
I felt from myself, I had to hide, so to everyone I lied.
Was embarrassed about my father, so I lied, and told them he died.
Many nights I locked myself inside of the bathroom and cried, because it's like I couldn't get it right no matter how hard I tried.
I feel extremely uncomfortable with these confessions.
But behind it, for you, there's a valuable lesson.
I'm thankful that I'm free because it truly is a blessing.
That I can write and be free, be myself for the world to see.
Because I'm tired of being more than me.

Inspired by a conversation with my brother about me being smarter and better than the average.

Dedicated to Rashaad , who never gave me his support through this journey, and I don't understand why but I know you love me.
June 6th, 2011.

I Really Do Love You

I love you. I mean, I really do love you. I love your smile,
I love your laughter, I love your hustle, I love your
confidence, I love your femininity mixed with your swag. I
love how you bite your lips and roll your hips when you're
feeling good about yourself. I hate your tears, I hate your
weakness, I hate those who've caused you pain, I hate to
see you hurting, I'm jealous of those who receive your
attention. I'm proud of you for not giving up, when giving
up would've felt so much better than holding on. I'm
thankful to have had you in my life. I'm appreciative to
have you now. I respect you for understanding my tears
when we would cry in the dark, lost in Central Park. I give
you my gratitude for holding me tight as a boy at night.
When I was misguided by the world and left alone to fight
it. I honor you for being my life jacket as I fought to swim
in the streets. If you close your eyes, you'll feel my love
with each heartbeat. So, when I say I love you, I really do
love you.

Inspired by writing her a letter with love, tears, smiles and
a bond unexplained between a brother and sister, who I
love like a mother.

Dedicated to P, 2011.

A Mother-In-Law

At fourteen lost in a cold world. Cold outside, so she let me into her warm home. Not just the weather, but outside seemed as if all the love was gone. The cold froze my tears, yet she warmed my heart. She still gave her love even when me and her daughter were apart. A young boy chasing a young girl, but just a boy trying to be more in a man's world. Arguments occurred and we'd even fight. All because that young boy couldn't get it right. No matter how hard I tried to seek the light, I was constantly roaming in the middle of the night. But back to this woman who understood my strife. I was lost into her first born, then our first was born. My decision to take a chance cause hearts to be torn and one left brutally scorned. It's not about us, but her, because she allowed us to love, live and learn. Also, my turn to yearn for love of her daughter. But just a boy, how could I ever get my life in order? Although, I'm not her daughter's brother, still she loved me like a son. There have been some after me. Still, I know I was treated like no other. So, I send my love and appreciation to my daughter's grandmother.

Inspired by love, growth, misunderstanding, and appreciation.

Dedicated to Ms. Velicia (Thank You). December 7th, 2011.

Love from the Core

A sister in soul, yet blood so far apart.
I remember you ever since I remember me.
I love you for understanding what I see.
You held my heart when I fell through.
How many people were there? Very few.
We've shared the same plate,
and almost lost it all when it was at stake.
You're a beautiful woman and one of the greatest I know.
You didn't have to tell me that you loved me because you let it show.
Me, your lil brother, shared the same loyalty from a mother.
From passing blunts to sharing dreams.
We had our faults, yet we're still a team.
I can't explain to you what you mean to me.
Never once when I showed up did you not open your door.
So just a brief note with love from the core.

Inspired by love, friendship, loyalty, and a love deeper than the streets.

Dedicated to Keaira Forever December 29th, 2011.

My Appreciation

A beautiful woman, yet deeper than the flesh.
More than an author, a strong black woman, determined
to do her best. Understand adversities from endurance,
patient, and a journey she overcame.
No one can say they feel her personal pain.
Triumphs and smiles fill her soul,
and although she's authored a book,
her real story hasn't been told.
Her ambition is worth more than gold.
I haven't met her, yet she warms hearts that're cold.
I know I'll write to get to my final destination.
I thank Assata for her inspiration.
I wrote this poem to show my appreciation.

Inspired by dreams coming true and our personal
definition of 'freedom' and how we value it.

Dedicated to Assata Shakur, October 28th, 2012.

Carlos

Truly a legend, one of the greatest that ever did it.
From St. Pete of Claver, to riding big.
You fell in love with her smile, then she gave you a kid.
We miss you for real.
 We shed tears but I only could imagine how Baby Doll and
Ms. Pat feel; Bookie still pour it up and sit down on the very
spot.
That occurred on Scott.
I was younger and didn't get the streets.
You said, "Save your money and keep new kicks on your feet."
We've had our misunderstandings due to them girls,
but one was my best friend while the other was my world.
Your smile set souls on fire in the hood,
even when we had nothing you taught us it was still all good.
You Bookie, Jason and Ball Bull paved the way from Scott to
Scott.
We miss you even if at times we don't show it,
but we send our love and stacks, we blow it.
Lil Moe get on that dirt bike and act a fool.
With that 125 you made it do what it do.
We love you hommie from C.P to T.P., from the West to
Robles,
from Duece to Jackson Height.
Continue to smile and shine bright.

Inspired by dreams and an old friend.

Dedicated to Carlos R. (R.I.P) April 7th, 2013.

T.J.M.S

I listen to you, but I hear him.
How he goes on and on about them.
Your laughter makes me smile inside,
but I can't let him see, so my smile I hide.
While he continues to make company to his deep misery.
I learn from you quoting Black History.
I ride in silence not sure what to say.
On my way to school, I deal with this every day.
I hate when the station fades because I hear more of him.
I'm only in the seventh grade.
How did his darkness become my shade?
The shade that is supposed to protect me.
So how could this be?
I learn about the world through your news,
and I can't wait to get older so I can go on your cruise.
I don't get why he constantly gives me the blues.
My flesh shows no sign, but spirit is deeply bruised.
How will I win if he continues to tell me that I'll always lose?
How you help me you'll never know,
how you help me through listening to you on the radio.
Even now you help me grow.
Thanks to the Tom Joyner Morning Show.

Inspired by hiding in a safe place.

Dedicated to Tom Joyner. April 12, 2017.

Spoken Words

Everywhere I go, everywhere I look I see the same thing.
I'm locked in prison and I'm going insane.
Finally, I realize it's time for a change.
I met an Angel in prison; she showed me how to believe in myself.
While her words took my breath.
I can't believe I met a poetess in this caged fortress.
She cried when I read her my poems, she felt my pain.
She's a poetess, I'm a poet, but we're not the same.
Beautiful like a free bird. Captured my heart with only spoken words.
The sweetest I've ever heard.
I hope I get to see her again,
and even one day we can become friends.
Showed me even though my burden is hard to lift.
That through it all I found my gift, and although I'm hurting.
As long as I believe. It'll get better for certain.
My own words had choken,
while her words came alive when they were spoken.

Inspired by seeing and hearing a beautiful, amazing, extraordinary Black Poetess who spoke at the prison.

Dedicated to Shacondria "Icon" Sibley. December 3rd, 2017.

Part II

Pieces of My Heart

Chapter 5: Her & Me

"The Lord is near to those who have a broken heart."

-Psalm 34:18

A Poem from Her
November 23rd on a Monday.

He was so misunderstood as a boy. Ran away as a child but didn't know what reality really meant until he was stuck in it. Burned bridges but didn't care because he found a new way to live by. He found the projects. Introduced to alcohol, drugs, & sex. Not knowing the consequences, he explored his sexuality. Met someone he thought he would be with forever but living in excitement & fast money plays its role. Got jammed up & the streets took her. She had his 1st beloved child, but sex excites everyone, love she lost for him. On his feet again and he met another. Turned him from a boy to a responsible adolescent. Still in that life of fast money, sex & drugs, he seen a lot, been through a lot yet still play. She had his 1st son. A Jr. Got so much to teach him yet he questioned his belongness of where he wanted to be. So, they started pulling apart. Still confused and undecided he searched for that one significant other he always thought and prayed about. He met a slightly younger girl. Was it lust or love? He wants to find out. 20 or 80? Emotionally and physically & spiritually on the same level but mentally not there. She didn't see him until she met his mind. 20 or 80 she was his 100. Still, they played. She played the innocent role and blind part until she couldn't no more. Friends & now lovers. Took her from a girl to a woman & she made that adult into a man & that Dad to a father. Planned their lives & their unborn. Pain & headaches came unexpectedly in their thought to be happy lives. She was pregnant with his "1st love child". Still addicted to sex & drugs and now a better life for his new family. He chose the wrong path to a better future. Captured in a world behind bars. Left so many behind as he struggles for a way out.

(Wrote this without thinking just wanted to see how it would come out, how do you like it?)

The 3 Of Us

It's like the love I have for you has its own life.
As if it's of its own being.
My love is not an emotion, it breathes deep breaths. It laughs, smiles and it even talks to me. I remember when we first met love it was standing, right beside you. You brought it to me. My stomach bubbled, my heart fluttered, and my words stuttered. Love scares me sometimes because I feel you don't want it around you anymore. I remember times when you would hold its hand so tight, or how we would share it in depths of passion. Never have I imagine the two of you being with another. Although we're far apart. We both speak to love, and I can't be with it if you're not with us. Considering without you love don't seem to come around. I want it to be with us forever. If our love ever dies, I'll know I held on to it with all the strength I could. Despite what adversities tried to come between the 3 of Us.

Inspired by love, fear, loneliness, separation, and falling in love with the closest friend I've ever had.

Dedicated to Her & Love. 2008.

A Note to my Love

I always wanted a devoted friend, someone who will be true to the end.
I know it don't seem fair, still I promise too always be there.
At times I know about me, you don't want to care.
Know that God wouldn't put too much on you that you couldn't bear.
I ask why? As you sit there and cry.
I swear I couldn't take if you decided to say goodbye.
Even though I'm in this prison life. Still, I'll honor you as my wife.
I promise to stop playing games, never again will I cause you pain.
Of course, what I say you want it to show.
I push the issue so you can know. I'm not going to lie.
Without you I don't know if I'll get by.
I'm a man now and I can be real
and tell you how I feel.
I love you as well as I can't wait to take that kneel.

Inspired by falling in love with my best friend.

Dedicated to Her. 2008

Only You Can Make Me Happy

On Meacham steps is where our words first met.
We would stick together similar to a duet.
I loved you with the same passion as Romeo loved Juliet.
 Our first date in Ybor City at the pizza place.
You set across from me with an innocent smile on your face.
You were young looking for a way out.
Ask me to show you what life's all about.
At first it was hard to get you, like rain in a drought.
Sixteen years you've been in Central Park,
told me "Even when the sunshine it still feels dark!"
Reminiscing on how I would stare at you while you take a nap.
Knowing in my heart I'd be the one who guides you like a map.
Your mother would beat on the front door.
As we would scramble to get all our clothes off the floor.
I knew that you loved me, because your mother demanded
you to stay away, still you came back for more. Holding you
close while I ask you your dreams. All you ask for was my last
name and a diamond ring. I think of the times we messed up
the sheets, or when you laughed at the noises I made at the
beach. Never would I imagine us apart. How could a man live
without his heart? I miss you so much and sometimes I get
sick on the stomach. Because no matter what the truth is, only
you can make me happy.

Inspired by the love I have for a friend.

I Regret

I know in life the things I've done has brought me to the point of meeting you. So, all those things I don't regret. But there are two things I regret. I regret only having one life to share with you. I regret only having one heart to give to you. I know if I could live longer, I could show you more and more of what you mean to me. I know if I had more hearts, I could give you more and more of my love. Since I only have one life to live, I'll live it with you. To give you the only heart I have. With giving you my heart, I'm giving you, my life. So, when my heart stops beating, I guess my life will be over. That's why I regret having one life and one heart.

Inspired by love and regret.

Dedicated to Her June 3rd, 2008.

Where is Yesterday?

It's almost as if we're playing hide and go seek, and I'm counting down and soon I'll find you. The love making, the smiles are captured by today and I pray we find yesterday in tomorrow. I think of how today was once our future, and yesterday we didn't plan this for today. I know love will continue to guide us and keep us strong. So, when you say we didn't plan this for today. It's just like asking me where is yesterday?

Inspired by broken dreams, love, patience, and friendship.

Dedicated to Her June 22nd, 2008.

A Flower

A loving relationship is like a beautiful flower that blooms with joy. It needs sunshine also rain to bloom into its greatest joy. Too much sun will burn it out. Too much rain will drown it out. With both comes deep firm roots, as well as understanding of receiving both to grow, and gain strength, and produce it's best from within. The sun shines after the dark.
Remember love is based on the perception of heart.

Inspired by going through relationships difficulties.

Dedicated Her. July 12th, 2008.

I Need You

You said you would die for me, but it seems like it's hard for you to live for me. Soon I'll be able to give you joy, laughter, and provide you with unselfish love that respects you.

I NEED YOU...
Your love is the cure for my loneliness, heart break, misunderstanding, and disbelief.

I NEED YOU...
I'm so scared I wish I could turn around and go back in time.
I'm here there's no turning back.

I NEED YOU...
In this journey ahead with the adversities know that I NEED YOU.

Inspired by love, loneliness, separation, and being in need.

Dedicated to Her. July 12th, 2008.

<u>Hearts</u>

The heart is the symbol of love,
as well as the origin of life.
Sometimes it's like craps throwing the dice to gamble.
Some hearts are like doors without any handles.
It can be pushed open and leave life floating,
or mind blown like a magical potion.
Some hearts are hard to open, like doors with bolt locks.
To open, it requires a lot of knocks.
My heart is the door, the lock is me,
and you're the one who holds the key.

Inspired by love.

Dedicated to Her July 14th, 2008.

Birthdays

May God bless you to be the woman he created you to be…

The mother you planned to be…

The wife you promised to be…

The friend you've learned to be…

Happy birthday.

Inspired by my love, future wife, co-parenting, and best friend's birthday,

Dedicated to her on her 20th birthday. December 15th, 2008.

At Times Love Is...

It hurts so bad, still at times it feels so great.
So strong, still at times it could break.
With it there's so much I could make.
Yet at times without it there's only so much that I could
take.
It's so confusing as if it's all an illusion.
Or at times when I'm so complete.
Which have me standing firm on my own two feet.
Bring me places I've yearned to explore
and feelings I've come to adore.
At times have me lost as a grain of sand at shore.
Love is many things, things that only we hold inside.
How we show it, receive it, or perceive it.
So, look within the depths of yourself to see what at times
love is...

Inspired by love, as well as what it could be.

Dedicated to Her. December 26th, 2008.

If Love Was... (Part 2)

If love was oxygen, I'd give you my last breath.

If love was living, I'd give you good health.

If love was a prize for you, I'd fight.

If love was light, I'd give you the sun that shines bright.

If love was faith, I'd be your hope.

If love was to be poor for you, I'd stay broke.

If love was laughter, I'd tell you a thousand jokes.

If love was a servant for you, I'd cater.

Since it's not I'll continue to express my love on this paper.

I try the best I can so my love for you I need you to please understand.

Inspired by a love to die for, as well as to live.

Dedicated to Her December 28th, 2008.

WHY Didn't you just Stay?

I love you for who you were, I hate who you've become.
Somewhere in my heart I know that we were meant to be.
As of right now it's so dark, that your love I can't see.
We both know things would've been so different if I was free.
Yet you told me you'd always love me unconditionally.
You still don't understand that…
That you're all I cared about that walked this land.
I was your man I was your number one fan!
What happen? Is this how it ends?
You left me as if I were nothing at all.
I always knew if things weren't right,
you'd be the one I could call. I scream so loud. "I HATE
YOU… I HATE YOU!"
As tears fall and my knees get weak. I close my eyes and
whisper "I love you… I really do love you." Hoping that
somewhere out there you could hear my heart cry out. Yet
would it even matter if you could. Because if you loved me and
wanted to be here for me you would. You were so bold, that's
what made my hear turn cold. Between our flaws there's a lot
left untold. As I lay and my thoughts drift in every way.
I wonder "Why didn't you just stay?
Inspired by love, a broken heart, and confusion.

Dedicated to Her. June 5th, 2009.

BROKEN HEARTS

I'm lost in a foreign place.
It's dark and the moon looks like a sad face.
The wind whispers like moans of pain.
Tears pour down from the sky like rain.
As I continue to wonder through this land,
I notice broken hearts everywhere.
Man after man I don't get it.
It's hard to understand.
In front of me is a lake.
It's years of crying from heartaches.
I see a man who didn't eat,
 or sleep he just cry, cry, and his tears continue to fill this lake.
A man lies in his bed and won't awake.
Because he's chasing his dream.
He sleeps, and sleep to catch his dream.
Still he's sleeping dreaming of the most beautiful
woman he's ever seen.
I see a line of men, millions waiting to see one doctor who
heals broken hearts.
Yet no one seems to have the right parts.
He looks like a child the age of nine.
He has been staring at her picture
for one hundred years crying.
There is a heart torn, and badly scorn.
How could someone do a heart that bad.
I put my hand to my chest knowing I did my best.
I thought all was fine,
until I came to realize this heart was mine.

Inspired by betrayal and a broken heart.

Dedicated to Her June 7th, 2009.

Say What You Need to Say

I'm listening, still I don't seem to hear you.
There's so much going on,
and you come back as if nothing went wrong.
All I wanted to hear is you apologize.
That would've made up for all my cries.
I don't want to hear your lies.
I love you, yet I don't like you anymore.
At one point you're all my heart would adore.
I'm not happy nor do I feel complete, as I did before.
I can go without you.
I'm stronger, and my heart has healed.
Now the truth within you have appeared.
You're selfish and living for yourself.
Still through all the pain.
I ask you to please say what you need to say!

Inspired by listening to her after she left when I needed
her most.

Dedicated to Her. June 22nd, 2009.

Mr. Emotional

They say emotions make you cry sometimes.
I say emotions make me ask why aren't my eyes drying?
Why do emotions have my heart dying?
She says it's my emotions, it's more about devotions and our foundation. Things come and things go, but love; true love will always grow.
It's so much more than words, it'll show.
What was to come she'll never know.
Still my emotions she'll see.
Because my emotions are a part of me.

Inspired by brokenness.

Dedicated to Her. July 9th, 2010.

How To Love

A butterfly taking flight away from the cocoon.
A woman now who've grown from an insecure girl.
Use to be afraid, now you face the world.
Have been to the moon and learned that anything too
bright burns.
Loved a boy looking deep into him for a man.
A rose that grew without thorns.
Was looking for someone with a way out.
Until you found it yourself.
You deserve happiness and the triumph for your trial and
error.
A diamond birthed in the worst conditions.
It's developed through pressure.
I was on a mission to show you how to love I just needed
you to listen.

Inspired by a woman who's in love with another man who
don't know how to love her.

Dedicated to Her 2011.

The Girl Who Changed My Heart

I smiled, she smiled, we smiled.
I laughed, she laughed, we laughed.
I cried, she cried, we cried.
I never knew love could be a non-contact sport.
I loved her way before intimacy was ever discussed between us.
Then when we did it, it was true passion fueled with love and imprisoned through trust.
I was an angry boy trapped in a man's body.
Never acknowledged all about what they said,
she listened to what he said, then looked at the moon.
Kissed him and laid in his bed.
She was the beauty, and I was the beast.
It was more than our words or flesh,
still our souls were destined to meet.
She wasn't scared of me; also, she could see the things I could see.
Although, they couldn't be seen with the naked eye.
She held my heart close, followed my lead, and never asked why.
One day I awaken to realize she had been taken.
Knowing within she couldn't have been faking.
I know it was sincere love making, I knew it wasn't an ordinary love.
She's out there somewhere, and constantly I wonder could I ever go back to the start.
With the girl who changed my heart.

Inspired by love, pain, and a bond that was shared between two hearts.

Dedicated to Her. April 2nd, 2011.

Happy Mother's Day

You know I may not acknowledge you on other holidays.
Because of the fact there's nothing I appreciate more
than the fact that you nurture my daughter with love,
laughter, and joy.
I thank you for being patient with her, and understanding
the value of parenthood, although through trial and error.
I salute you with honor, and respect.
I love you for giving my baby life,
and even though I'm not there in your lives.
I thank you with my life.
I don't have the ability to show you in any other way.
Other than giving you my respect on Mother's Day.

Inspired by being a co-parent and being absent.

Dedicated to Her. April 20th, 2011.

<u>Thinking About You</u>

If you're angry at me and I'm drowning, would you
pretend not to see?
If I made a mistake and called, you a bitch would you
forgive me?
Would you write if I were scheduled to die and never be
free?
Could you love me forever even when we're old?
If so, then we share a story that must be told.
I feel like a freed bird with the wind under my wings.
When I feel all the love and joy that you bring.
I'm in a very dark place, at times feel as though I'm lost
without a trace.
As if I'm bound and no one is seeking for me to be found.
My love is a gift, and my loyalty comes with honor.
I envision you from different eyes than the rest of the
world.
I love the thought of you, to me you're precious like a
pearl.
Don't run away, please don't go astray.
I'll be there one day.
What is in it for the two of us share.
No one else could ever compare.

Inspired by wanting her to be around.

Dedicated to Her. 2011.

Introducing Our Conclusion

I wonder what song could explain,
or what taste could describe how she makes me feel.
What fragrance is similar or what texture comes close to her touch.
I've explored the dictionary A to Z, still I can't find a word that defines
how I feel about her. We've been there and of course we've done that.
Yet we continue to try repeatedly. She doesn't want to talk but she continues to listen.
We didn't finish, so we started over. I ask her for her name.
She looks at me and realize how much we've change.
As I reminisce on our past.
I know things will never be the same.
We all notice the picture yet disregard the frame.
She's different now because she's a woman.
I'm different now because I'm a man.
We shared something that no-one else will ever understand.
I wish her well in this life.
Knowing one day she'll be a wonderful wife.
A good wife to someone.
Hopefully, she'll forgive me for all the wrong that I've done.
Just to clear up all the confusion allow me to introduce our conclusion.

Inspired by understanding, letting go, love, dried tears, and starting over.

Dedicated to Her. June 6th, 2011.

Love. Faith. Devotion.

It's not easy saying something that will change everything forever.
Knowing it won't make it better.
Amid pleasures that causes pain, guilt is the last thing on your mind.
Not aware that it will come to light in due time.
There's a want and there's a need.
I'd die for who'll live for me.
Her kiss is my freedom, my touch is her temptation.
We'd ride side by side, standing strong with pride.
Love is deeper than the words that's spoken, like oil pipes in the ocean. Honor is devotion as Faith is what keep our lives in motion.
She can't see me or be held by the one man who holds her heart.
So, she goes on with another knowing how it would end from the start.
I could never grasp hold of that part.
Dreams become fantasies that you pray one day come true.
There're so many emotions held in that she never knew.

Inspired by love, faith, devotion being absent.

Dedicated to Her. June 10th, 2012.

Untold

When I thought I knew it all, all I knew was nothing.
I was so angry because I was so hurt.
I was so mean because I was so scared.
I laughed with everyone, because alone I cried.
I just want to be free, free of all the chains.
I hold on now because I know I can't let go.
Yet the things I let go helped me grow.
The mirror isn't the only place I see my reflection.
It's in the three who are so different yet share one connection.
In my heart they have their own section.
There're pieces of myself that haven't been broken and are still whole.
My heart has been shattered, but I keep a peaceful soul.
All that 'hurt and can't heal' is a part of the mold.
Despite all that I write, still there's so much that goes untold.

Inspired by writing a letter to Her and sharing my thoughts and feelings. June 10th, 2011.

She Just Doesn't Understand

Faith is blind and love is gullible,
so, we fantasize of living like the Huxtables.
But reality kicks in when you're calling her, but he
answers.
And despite all the questions, she gives you no answer.
You tell yourself she's still young, so she just doesn't
understand.
Or it's because you left her out there without a helping
hand.
So why wouldn't she seek comfort from another man?
As the years went by, and countless tears were shed,
and all the yelling about how you wish she were dead.
You talk with a little more sense so you can share with
her your two cents. You give a lifetime of "I'm different
now" all in fifteen minutes.
Until at the end of the call she doesn't respond to your "I
love you's,"
So, your feelings are now hurt again, and despite your
genuine sincerity,
and that she is the one that gives true clarity.
Still, she just doesn't understand.

Inspired by loving someone who don't love me back.
December 17th, 2012.

A Blind Heart

I fell hard and was looking for you to catch me.
Yet you were nowhere I could see.
You were supposed to have my back.
You allowed the world to get us off track.
I can't point the finger at you,
because I can't say what I would do.
No that's a lie and so not true.
My love for you would've never stop this you knew.
The strange thing is how apart we've grew.
One thing I know for sure,
is you can count on love when it's pure.
Yeah, I know things go with the average,
which I felt we were so far from. Yet your love is a
fraction to some.
Because if you loved me, even despite what you do.
I should always be able to count on you.
Especially in times like this.
Your words would be soothing like a gentle kiss.
But my well-being wasn't on your hearts to do list.
I sometimes wonder am I ever missed.
I wish you well and now my heart can see because I've
removed the veil.

Inspired by love lost and love once cherished.
February 10th, 2013.

Broken Wings

Awakening from a dream of us failing to complete a love scene.
But it's not hard as it seems.
I guess that comes from reminiscing on the past.
Yeah, we smile, but of course it's a part of our mask.
 I can't seek love that don't want to be found.
You love me but not in love, now come on, how does that sound?
This is what the heart must go through.
We did things that we were supposed to never do.
But I blame me for leaving you.
I wish I could right wrongs. Since I can't, instead I just write my wrongs. There's only so much the heart brings, and then there's only so far we can go with broken wings.

Inspired by real love. February 15th, 2013.

Not Mine

When I'm weaken by my strengths, and the things that makes me smile makes me cry.
Understand that all I can do is try.
Realizing its rain that helps roses grow.
It's not always about holding on but letting go.
Just because you're clean doesn't mean you're pure.
When you accept love, you should be sure.
Learning with love they'll be times we must endure.
Bombs explode in the heart knowing true love would last from the start. Loss of breath, Love in the midst of death.
I would've held you for ten lifetimes.
As I lay here alone still, I can't believe you're not mine.

Inspired by love and love lost. 2014.

Not Friends

Pain heals in time, they say.
But this pain hurts the worst way.
It tears me apart, this pain you've cause my heart.
I sit and fantasize about being free.
Others are amazed at the effect you have on me.
I respect your decision,
and I assume it was inspired by me being in prison.
I think back over all these years of all that I've been missin.'
When you told me to stay home, I should've listened.
This year is ending.
And again, another year has come to past and we're still not friends.

Inspired by thinking about her and how close I am to freedom. December 12th, 2017.

Part III
Pieces of My Mind

Chapter 6: My Thoughts & Me

"Commit your works to the Lord, and your thoughts will be established."

-Proverbs 16:3

It's All Over

As I close my eyes I can see the light,
knowing I never could get it right.
I hear so many voices,
contemplating on all the bad choices.
In life we have so many fears,
and constantly flowing with tears.
As I get closer to the light, I notice the flames.
Hopefully, the fire will burn away the pain.
As I take my last breath, I realize I wasn't ready for death.
Now the malice, agony and hatred are gone.
There's no more fear, no more tears, because now, it's
all over.

Inspired by thoughts of suicide and life. May 29th, 2003.

Against All Odds

I look up and see the skies,
still gazing deep, I see a beautiful kingdom.
Streets made of gold.
There's love, peace and no hearts are cold.
It's a kingdom where no one is crying,
no pain or suffering.
But as I look into the world, I see people hurting deep
down inside.
People tell me to maintain yet fail to see all the frustration
captured in my brain. Lord, I see your beautiful home.
Why, God, is it taking me so long?
One day I know I'll be there.
 For now, down here there's only so much I can bear.
I try so hard, for now, I'm against all odds.

Inspired by having faith and being ready to see the truth.
May 29th, 2003.

I'm Aware You Think I'm Not

Over the years I've learned to stay out of trouble's way.
So, I can grow old and watch the grandchildren play.
That's why I give love to my kids every day.
I ask God for forgiveness, wisdom and understanding
every time I pray.
I pay close attention to the world around me because I
know it's fake.
The smiles and laughter hold poison like a rattlesnake,
So the more I live,
I become stronger, I become wiser, I become greater...
and I'm aware you think I'm not.

Inspired by friends becoming foes and growth. 2008.

That's Just My Baby Momma

She just works eight hours a day for my child.
She just sacrifices buying herself clothes to buy my kid clothes.
She just pays the rent by herself.
She just makes sure they eat every day.
She just makes sure every holiday and birthday my child has a smile.
She just comes through for my child every time I let them down.
Oh yeah, that's just my baby Momma.

Inspired by observations, experience, and my baby mommas who I'm proud of.

Dedicated to the women who gave birth to
"My Adorable 3'. June 12th, 2008.

Crack

It came in the summer of 1985. When it came, so much was deprived.
I can remember at thirteen when I first met crack on the scene.
I couldn't believe this little piece of crack,
would make this grown woman lay on her back.
Small as a sunflower seed, it would make a grown man beg and plead.
It destroyed lives, made husbands leave their children and wives.
Families living in homes with no hot water.
Would you believe that crack made mothers sell their daughters?
I was blind, in the dark, until I was exposed to Central Park.
Crack affected not just the dealers or users.
It turned people into abusers.
Young boys selling crack, and skipping school,
because all the young girls thought all the dope boys were cool.
It deteriorated homes; as I got older, I realized why my father was gone.
It's not the high, or profit, but the lifestyle alone.
I know for a fact, there isn't too much that has influenced us like crack.

Inspired by losing my father to crack and observations.

Dedicated to those who've been touched one way or another.
June 15th, 2008.

A Man's Life and Chess

A man's life is like a patient game of chess.
Every move has to be your best.
You've got to be five moves ahead of the one being
made.
Some moves will be made in order to make sacrifices.
But too many sacrifices become losses,
and like a chain you're only as strong as your weakest
link.
So even with making a move with the pawn you must
think.
The king is the most valuable piece.
Yet the Queen is the most respected.
Master the game of chess and you'll understand a man's
life.

Inspired by chess moves and plans for life. July 12th,
2008.

<u>Doing My Best</u>

I was contradicted,
I was doing wrong trying to be optimistic.
I'm special. I got hand-picked to go through life's
devastations.
The more I feel the more I'm contemplating on my
destination,
instead of observation.
Growth gave me maturity and allowed me spiritual purity.
 Learned not to hate, and how to thank God for the
blessings the Devil can't take,
as well as handling it like a man the things put on my
plate.
Things have gotten better, in fact, they have gotten great.
In this journey I've found my fate.
This isn't really about emotions but devotions
and what life has in motion.
I'm not settling for less or concerned about the rest.
I'm just doing my best.

Inspired by life experiences, challenges, a visit from
mother and just doing my best. July 13th, 2008.

Keep Trying

My childhood went astray,
left home so I guess I was a runaway.
I was hungry so I didn't have time to play.
I was surviving in the worst way.
At age fifteen I had my first baby.
That's when things started getting crazy.
I was lost, didn't quite know the streets came with a big cost.
Late nights, cold bitten, while my momma's prayers kept my soul fightin.
I wonder like Stevie why I couldn't see,
knowing in my heart there were places I'd rather be.
It was burdensome; still I had to do me,
even with the world doing fine. While I'm locked down, doing time
and thinking about my kids crying.
Something inside touched me and said, 'Keep trying.'

Inspired by struggles. July 14th, 2008.

Me, Myself, and I

As I listen to Myself, I ask Me who he is.
Myself is confused and doesn't know Me.
I learned to understand Me,
but I see Myself being misunderstood when
I share things with Myself.
It gives Me a deeper understanding to grasp hold onto.
Sometimes I am captured by Myself and won't let Me go.
The thoughts I have are deep like the ocean.
A hundred-year-old oak tree isn't as strong as Me.
Looking into Myself, seeking something great with faith.
Once Me, Myself and I start the evolution of becoming
one,
then I will know Me and understand Myself and be free.

Inspired by soul searching and seeking a deeper cause.
December 12th, 2008.

My Generation

It's complicated trying to put relevant knowledge in your head.
It's like trying to put it in with no lubrication.
That's because most of you are fabrication.
I'm uncut, like way back when they were free basin.'
Now they're lacin' and still chasin.'
Not aware so you all are gettin' hit without bracin.'
That's because you're moving without contemplation.
Your lives are based on misappropriation.
You've got to recognize what they're doing: mutation.
You're sleep with your eyes wide open.
Please wake up to see what they have in motion.
You all think alike, so obtuse.
You're concentrated like apple juice.
I can't say you're sorry, you're just tardy.
You're dead before you're dying, so loquacious.
That's why you don't see what's right in your faces.
I'll lead and continue to proceed.
I'm trying to keep my concentration.
So, I can guide my generation.

Inspired by my generation.

Dedicated to my generation. June 8th, 2009.

I'm Just Living

The man in the mirror is the real contender. I stay focused so my kids can have a hot dinner and wear warm clothes in the winter. Labeled a thug, but still, I ask God to forgive me for my sins. Because I'm aware he's, my friend. I travel so high just to see, knowing where I'm going, also who I'll be. Aware that this life's negativity comes with a severe fee. Like losing my life or my dream girl. She was supposed to be my wife. I've come to realize in that game; this is the price. See, we dream, and we live, we fall, and we get up; sometimes we don't. The key is to learn from your mistakes. Live to be happy, be all you can be. I'm going to give it all I've got, to gain all that's given, because I'm just living.

Inspired by being isolated and just living. June 8th, 2009.

Define Woman

When you look into the mirror, what do you see?
Okay, you have beautiful eyes, your hair is healthy
and your lips are perfect. But do you see substance or
intelligence?
Can you see the truth, the real you?
How you see yourself determines the quality of yourself
mentally, spiritually, physically, and emotionally.
What you believe about yourself is what will manifest in
your lives.
I want all you mothers, daughters, sisters, and wives, to
listen to me,
see what I see, be all you can be.
Give it all you possess and let that manifest.
Look within and understand to be defined you don't need
a man.
You're everything, you're a woman who brings life as well
as love from the womb all the way to the tomb.
When it's all said and done, you're still a woman.

Inspired by observing women of all calibers. June 9th,
2009.

Get Away

I distance myself for the best of my health.
It's not easy trying to obtain great wealth.
I'm trying to possess it and avoid an early death.
So, I understand the essence of my breath.
They say we forget about where we come from.
How could that in any way be?
Honestly, where I came from forgot about me.
Just went on as if I was debris.
In this world everything has a price; nothing is free.
Yet we go on and on about being real and being down.
Then again, that's only if I'm on top wearing the crown.
A smile is just a frown upside down.
To each his own, that's why I strive to have my own.
Because I'm a man who has grown.
Where were you when I was alone?
It does seem long; you didn't even answer your phone.
That's unimportant and now I don't care.
Right now, it doesn't matter.
As for now I'm just taking it day by day, so I can get
away.

Inspired from those who stop believing in me while
incarcerated. June 9th,2009.

Do They Really Feel Me?

Do they really feel me?
I sit and observe the two read what I wrote,
wondering would they take me as a joke,
or feel me and give me hope.
As I analyze their demeanor and see their expressions,
I assume they're feeling my confessions.
I can recognize that they come from two different roads.
This stop here will be a part of the three of our molds.
Their eyes are roaming across my written words
and they're deep in thought.
Probably about their families and destruction in their own lives,
realizing it's their fault.
They look at me different now.
These two men, and I talk man-to-man.
Now I feel they understand.
As they read, they see a part of their lives in some way.
Just with words, they couldn't say.
They tell me they feel me, but do they really feel me?

Inspired by observing two men read what I wrote while incarcerated. June 13th, 2009.

I Wonder What He Wonders

I wonder what it feels like to have bombs exploding while I'm sleeping or being tortured and held against my will. To watch my mother, sister, wife, or daughter be raped and tortured. To be told that what I've believed all my life is wrong and a lie. I wonder what I would do if I was being robbed and considered a terrorist in my homeland. To not be able to feed my children or watch them develop a hateful mind state. I wonder what would possess me to kill thousands of innocent people, let alone kill myself to seek a superior being with all I hold inside. I wonder what it is to endure centuries of pain. I wonder what he wonders...

Inspired by being in a cell next to a suspected terrorist, listening and being heard.

Dedicated to all those who wonder. June 15th, 2009.

All That's Shown

Standing in the pouring rain, trying to cleanse my soul.
Being baptized in God's tears allows me to put away my
fears. Understanding and wisdom are to be sought until
death.
But some things will never be understood, even at our
last breath. Confusion and the lack of wisdom; that's
what causes a delusion.
They'll enter our minds only to lose control over the one
thing that controls everything.
When the heart hurts there's no worse pain.
Realizing it's the opposite of the minority who defines
insane.
'Who am I?' is a popular question that goes without
answer.
Another one is 'how can a six-year-old die from cancer?,'
or 'how can someone who holds my heart break it apart?'
It's not lust, but affection alone.
It's not about what if, but all that's shown.

Inspired by all that's shown. July 30th, 2012.

Time

Just wanted to talk to you for a second.
I know you're unbelievably valuable.
I wish somehow you could slow down when it comes to
my kids.
My oldest looks like a little woman, because of you.
My son became aware of my absence because you
continued to go on. And at times I swear you were
moving like we were in a race, or some moments you
were moving at a snail's pace.
You've taught me a great lesson, so I slowed down on
the stressin.'
Some don't acknowledge you until we're forced to watch
the clock, or when it's too late and for them you won't
stop.
I've learned to value you increasingly as you go by.
By now I finally realize what counts at the end of day as
we unwind.
It's you, all the time.

Inspired by time and absence.

Dedicated to all the time that has come and gone, and
the time ahead of me. September 27th, 2012.

Lady Justice

I don't think you're blind I just feel like you don't want to
see,
because only if you would open your eyes so many of us
would be free.
How could it be you whom we can honestly trust?
When you continue to let them get away with killing us.
That's why change is a must.
It's our communities who're blind and don't know.
That you're in love with an old man name Jim Crow.
 After being in your presence they don't want to give us
jobs.
But I guess it's better than when you'd deliver us to lynch
mobs.
The scale you hold is off balance,
and not equal so you don't treat us the same.
We cried tears when thanking God for Obama who said,
"It's time for a change!" But you're the one to blame.
Open your eyes, stop telling all these lies.
Since your blind don't you hear our cries?! .
Open your hand and feel the tears we've shed.
PLEASE! PLEASE! Can't you see too many of us are
dead?
You're not blind, you just look the other way.
Lady justice can you hear me or are you claiming to be
deaf too?
You can't imagine the things that we go through.
All because the things that you fail to do.

Inspired by being a victim of America's failing judicial
system, and the murder of Philander Castile. "R.I.P
PHILANDER."

Dedicated to Black America. June 9th, 2017.

Chapter 7: My Feelings & Me

"A fool has no delight in understanding, but in expressing his own heart."

-Proverbs 18:2

The Enemy

The enemy is not a White man nor what region you feel
is against you.
It's not the police, laws, or prosecutors.
The enemy is not those who've done you wrong.
The enemy is the lack of dignity and respect.
The enemy is no self-control or understanding of self.
The enemy is within in.

Inspired by the enemy. July 10th, 2008.

The Souls of My Sisters

My mother has four boys: not one sister in the home.
Indeed, there was a strong, dedicated, respected, loving,
and understanding sister: my mother.
Behind that great big smile is pain, misunderstanding,
anger, loneliness, and abandonment. As I grow to mature
and understand the souls of my sisters, it is something as
men we need to acknowledge.
I read about Black Women because God knows I love me
a Black woman. I've learned more than just how they
liked to be pleased.
I've learned why at times they cry, why they smile, why
they strive so hard. I understand their short-comings and
their triumphs.
It's so much we must discover about our women.
Despite the old saying 'the ways of a woman are
unknown.'
That's because the souls of my sisters are unshown.

Inspired by observations and becoming my mother's
friend.

Dedicated to all women who overcome. July 11th, 2008.

<u>Growth</u>

One of the most important things in life, I've learned, is to grow.
Grow mentally, spiritually, and emotionally.
Grow in maturity, grow in education, and grow in your career.
Growth is important for us as people who seek change for a greater cause. Growth keeps us standing tall and to get up every time we fall.
Growth is life.

Inspired by growing. July 12th, 2008

Freedom

Sitting here listening to my thoughts, watching the rain throw itself against the window while the thunder screams aloud.
Wondering do the trees feel captured by the earth, as I do to this cell. Looking at the bird that soars, trying to dodge the rain in a storm.
Doing so is like throwing rocks at the ground trying to miss.
The wind whispers, brushing against the tree, but it's locked into the ground.
As it rains harder, I think even outside this cell window, is there really freedom.

Inspired by thoughts of freedom, incarceration, patience, and awareness.

Dedicated to me and the bird that soared. June 15th, 2008.

<u>Holding On</u>

I've been places not just in the physical form.
Mentally, spiritually, and emotionally I've been through a storm.
Although, I'm down I refuse to go under, I refuse to drown.
Sometimes you must allow things to work themselves out.
I accept my surroundings and use it to my advantage.
Self-preservation is the strength of my observation.
I know my circumstances comes from me taking certain chances.
So, although I'm down, I'll keep doing what I'm doing to maintain
and keep my head afloat.
I've got this life jacket for now.
Still in time, I'll be the captain of the boat.

Inspired by thinking of a way out, knowing there will be better days.
June 13th, 2009.

The Unknown

I don't like to be told I'm wrong when I know I'm right.
I don't want to hear that I'm being sentimental when I'm hurting.
I know morality is within, yet for our own purpose we allow it to bend.
I've learned that just because we're kin doesn't mean you're my friend. Also, just because it's important to me doesn't mean it's important to you. Don't judge me for what has been but for what I'll do.
I've indulged in things you've never knew.
A young boy lost in a forest they call a world.
Mind captured by wickedness as a clam captures a pearl.
Although, I was thirteen I wanted to kill myself, and destroy my soul.
Was it because of the things I wasn't taught?
Or maybe things within that weren't sought?
Is the smile mischievous for hiding deep pain?
Or me not telling due to the shame?
Who am I? Who was I? Who will I become?
Will I run or face it alone?
We've got to look deep within us and take hold of the unknown.

Inspired by going years without disclosing my shame and sexual abuse.

Dedicated to all those who held it in. 2008.

What If...

What if you could change the color of the sky or make the choice if birds could fly?

What if you had the power to choose whether we live or die?

What if you could get to ask God one why?

What if you could set a nation of people free?

What if everything you do, someone disagree?

What if this? What if that? Most what ifs are regrets. We dream when we want, we create when we want. What if? Still, with whatever's said and done, thought or planned, dreamed, or fantasized, really, what if...?

Inspired by what if? June 29th, 2009.

<u>Shoeless</u>

He's only four years old and he's outside with no shoes on. And it's so cold. When I see him, I think of my son, wondering what this little boy could have done. He's only a baby, yet the life he's trapped in so crazy. His big brothers are lost, so he gets the short end of the stick and pays the cost. Both of his parents are physically disabled. Living in poverty with that; it's part of the home being unstable. But the two of them do the best they can; the father, to me, is a good man. They call him 'Shoeless' as a nickname. Still, I don't think they quite feel his pain. His nose is runny, and all the other kids think he's funny. I guess we're all product of our environment in one way or another. I knew a little boy who smiled, cried, laughed, ran, chased, played, and grew shoeless.

Inspired by all the kids who roamed without shoes in Central Park and every ghetto in the world.

Dedicated to Lil Shoeless from Central Park. July 2nd, 2009.

My Eleven and a Half's

I can't say what life's been for you or even the things
you've been through. There're so much my eyes have
witnessed.
I'm twenty-three and back then I never would've
imagined the things I'd see.
I know that now it all made me. I'm a father, I'm a son,
and a friend.
Yet no one can say they've been where I've been.
You may have been touched by a monster, may have
experienced the same journey,
and even used the same attorney.
Although, we've shared the same path,
I doubt you could fill my eleven and a half's.

Inspired by my life experiences. July 2nd, 2009.

<u>Hunger Pains</u>

Never would I have thought I'd close my eyes and endure
hunger pains.
These feelings would drive the average person insane.
You don't know the effect they bring.
Abandoned as a child I experienced these feelings a few
nights.
People would eat right in front of me without offering me
a bite.
My strength from my past experiences destroyed the
dark with the light.
Now as I lay up late, I think of enjoying a home cooked
plate. I'm locked up in this cell and there's nothing for me
to eat.
As a man it makes me feel weak.
Thinking of the times I spent in the streets, age fourteen,
standing on my own two feet.
There's one thing I hate I had to meet, that disturbs my
brain
that's these hunger pains.

Inspired by being hungry. July 4th, 2009.

A Part of Me

To the world:
I want you to seek my understanding like an Amber Alert
searching for a lost girl.
Why I think the way I do is a question they'll ask you.
Even those who've known me forever never knew.
Many things will be said and done,
but you'll be so far away. Still, you'll feel me like the sun.
I pray these traits pass on to my daughters and my son.
I'll touch souls one way or another.
She let me down yet now she's a good mother.
Dreams were broken and goals were failed.
Even in the free world we could feel captured in a cell.
When we play in the dark, we learn to see without light,
and just because it's dark doesn't mean it's night.
You'll feel me whether it's good or bad,
even if I made you smile or made you sad.
If you knew me or wish you had.
Continue to see what you see,
knowing eventually, you'll possess a part of me.

Inspired by understanding and a hunger to be
understood. July 30th, 2009.

Losing It

I know what I'm doing is wrong. I'm contemplating on being disciplined for my actions.
I need to give my ego a little satisfaction.
I'm so…something that I can't explain.
My desire to break free is untamed.
I've run away, searching for something or someone to blame. As I sit here in this cell, just me alone.
I capture myself in another zone.
Remember, there will be many things occurring that will be unknown,
don't add up and don't fit.
I share this with you during losing it.

Inspired by pain and confusion. September 7th, 2009.

<u>Writing in the Dark</u>

I feel so empty, yet I'm full of hatred.
My mother says if I keep it up, I won't make it.
I realize when handling a heart,
there's no easy way to break it.
I smile, still I know I'm faking it.
I did so many things.
To be honest, I knew this is what it would bring.
All those reckless decisions.
Got me staring in prison.
We all have so many problems.
But we have our own way of trying to solve them,
not really analyzing what caused them.
A peace of mind will come in due time.
First, I need y'all to stop acting blind.
Because I know all of you can see,
see what's hurting inside of me.
I know that with overcoming all that I've suffered,
one day I'll be free.

Inspired by writing in the dark while hurting. December
28th, 2009.

Fed Up

I know who I am, also who I once was, as well as who
I'll become. I've endured an extreme amount of pain.
Still, I fight myself to maintain.
They do things, assuming they're getting away.
Knowing they couldn't imagine the madness captured within
me; they'll go crazy if, within, I let them see.
I'm tired of being taken as a joke,
to a point where it's hard to breathe, so I choke,
my soul is filled with anger
from looking into the mirror, seeing a stranger. I'm lost, yet I'm
found. Found because I'm bound behind this wall. God reveals
things to me, then some things I'm left to figure out. Like, why
is Jason dead? Why am I in the Feds? And why a teenage boy
decided to open my seven-year-old daughter's legs? I don't
get it or is it not for me to get. Then I think when I'm dead and
gone will I ever be forgotten. I wish sometimes I could talk to
my dad, also be one to my kids like the one I never had. I
guess right now I'm mad, even sad. But most of all, I'm fed up.

Inspired by pain, hate, tears, lost love, misunderstanding and a
journey.

Dedicated to Alex (Big Perm) who told me to stay strong.
October 24th, 2010.

Tears in the Mirror

Young, ambitious, and a charmer all captured inside a
boy transitioning into a man.
To become everything his heart is set out to be.
The man that society wasn't prepared for.
Only to be deprived of his freedom.
To look into a mirror to see his kid's father,
his mother's first born, his little brother's keeper,
also, the man women believed in. Hungry for
understanding, thirsty for vengeance and a prayer for
salvation.
Which is all a mixture that fuels his smiles as well as his
tears. To realize that fearlessness is power, power is
purity
and purity is godly.
Looking into those tears in the mirror shows a reflection
of the things gone unseen.
Yet the heart and soul can witness it clear as a sunny
day. You'll never forget what you see in the tears in the
mirror.

Inspired by life, tears, and looking into a mirror.
November 11th, 2010.

The Man I Met in Prison

One day I was walking, looking around as this man said,
'I've been searching for you, now I've found you.'
I stared at him for a while, confused.
Still, I continued to walk and listen, not wanting to be rude.
He talked about God and how he loved his three kids.
He wasn't entertained by foolishness and didn't disrespect
women.
Also, too steadfast, he did what it took.
He was young, still he listened, understood, and read books.
He was patient, humble and aware of what was occurring in
the Middle East.
He shared with me how he was once lost and couldn't stand
on his own two feet.
He was charismatic, well-spoken and had good manners.
I didn't understand how this man was once considered an
animal.
We went on and on for hours about everything from politics to
health, to attaining great wealth.
Someone called my name, yet this man answered.
Then I realized this man was me, it was my decision to
become aware of the man I met in prison.

Inspired by growing, facing the enemy, and becoming a man in
prison.

Dedicated to all those who transformed into better men and
better women captured in a cage. March 31st, 2011.

Always Thinking

Thinking of the times I was hungry so I would go snatch a purse.
How I smile, still sometimes waking up seems worse.
Feeling like all I've been through I've got to be cursed.
Unanswered questions like why my mother chose him and I was around first.
Even the first child she birthed. Not understanding after all these years why I continue to hurt.
She says I need to let it go, but she just doesn't know.
Why would a thirteen-year-old boy contemplate taking his own breath?
Feeling like he's closer to death.
People say go to God, but that's the same God who told her to put her husband before me.
So how could He understand if He says that's the way it ought to be?
Thinking of old times and the old saying 'out of sight, out of mind.' That doesn't mean for you to act like you're blind.
I can't give up, so I'll keep trying.
I love my kids as well as their mothers.
Well, you know me, always thinking.

Inspired by thoughts that I have. April 3rd, 2011.

Tampa Park

Running around playing Cops and Robbers,
walking to 15th Street to get in the pool, doing good,
having fun, making good grades in school, wearing the latest
Jordans, Hilfiger, and Polo, of course, I was cool.
Couldn't go play ball until all my chores were done.
She would smile every time I hit a homerun.
To my house everyone came,
because I was the kid with all the new video games.
I could look out my bedroom window and see the GTE building
glow.
I used to check myself to make sure I was 'fly.
before the young girls of Tampa Park would walk by.
My mother's friends would rub my face and call me handsome;
I used to be shy.
Some nights I'd hear crying from the fighting with my brother's
father, behind her room door.
"I can't get in the door it's locked! What did she do?"
Not knowing, he was strung out on crack.
I had a plan to be her hero, so she didn't need a man.
Tears were shed during the dark.
This is what I remember about Tampa Park.

Inspired by memories and broken dreams, dedicated to my
mother.

Dedicated to All the OG's in Tampa Park who never influenced
me to do wrong. Nard, T-One, Cage, Troy and R.I.P 69,
Goldie, Sean.

Nightmares

Closed eyes, yet I still see.
See the things trapped inside of me.
Although I'm not free I know where I want to be.
I try so hard, yet my dreams are torn apart.
Scared to go to sleep,
not aware of what I'll meet.
Screaming, fighting, and trying to get away.
Not understanding why or how this happened,
even after I pray.
Trying to contain my soul from going astray.
Awakening in the wee hours of the night,
barely catching my breath.
Seconds from being scared to death.
Not aware of the stares.
All this due to my nightmares.

Inspired by being scared to sleep. April 30th, 2011.

The More I Try

I don't understand the things I believe in,
yet I believe in the things that I don't understand.
Some say pain is pleasure, yet pleasure isn't pain.
There's so much I've seen. I endure so much,
and I feel like I lose all that I touch.
I'm so tired of being in prison,
but not just in the physical form. My mind, my heart and
my soul are living through hell waiting to unfold.
So many feelings that can't be told.
It's hard to explain why I cry.
Still, it seems like the more I try…

Inspired by being anxious, tired of being in prison, and
holding on. May 2nd, 2011.

Proverbs Hidden in Plain View

The more I read I learn different words.
Like the ones I've never heard.
I quietly whisper the songs of the caged bird.
I take time out for meditation to avoid medication.
To help me with life and reconciliation.
My faults I do embrace with an understanding grace.
Wisdom to the soul is like water in a drought.
Also, the sunshine will always dry out the flood.
A friend is better than a brother who shares the same blood.
Don't make a final decision based on what the heart envisions.
In your hand grasp the wind.
If you can do that, allow your enemy to become your friend.
Some sons will desire the likeness of their mothers.
While some despise their brothers.
People cause pain as well as kill,
just to make others relate to how they feel.
Everything you understand isn't meant to be understood.
A wife should honor her husband.
Also, a husband should please his wife.
Be delicate with her heart.
Vengeance will be the incentive of the woman's heart that's
torn. Music is soothing, also influential.
Remain stable to direct your complete potential.
Listen, also please take heed,
so that in this journey of life you will proceed.

Inspired by experience. May 9th, 2011.

It Is What It Is

I'm asleep, yet I'm awake.
I'm walking, yet I'm not on my own two feet.
I'm a winner, although I can be beat.
There are things that need to be found so I seek.
We often ponder about what tomorrow will bring.
But do we ever think about what yesterday has left?
Some things are taken. Some things are given,
even at times you are not willing.
I read and I write.
I turn the other cheek; still, I fight.
I fight the things that try to hide my light.
I bathe, still I'm not clean.
I'm not clean yet I'm pure.
I believe, I don't understand.
I give respect because I want it to reflect.
 All those who I disrespect, I apologize with much regret.
I will continue to live, because at the end of the day,
it is what it is.

Inspired by thoughts of things that occurred and things
yet to come. May 25th, 2011.

The Wickedness That Lies

I've walked in those shoes on your feet, for a long time.
I understand where they've taken you, but all will be fine.
Just pay attention to the path and all its signs.
Don't think you've got to run fast as you can to get there.
You'll miss so much, and they'll be times
you feel you've lost touch. Bruises heal
and despite what they say no one truly
can understand how you feel.
Most won't respect you being real.
Unless they're continuing to get
something out of the deal.
But to be a monster in disguise takes craft and skill.
They'll betray you to the point you'll want to kill.
So, understand most of your future foes
are your friends right now.
I see you looking at them naively asking how?
Pain hurts, but recovery wouldn't feel so good
if you didn't feel the pain.
And how can we appreciate sanity if we never witness the
insane.
As well as being grateful of the sunshine because we've
experienced the pouring rain.
Love spoken and love shown is nowhere near the same.
Instead of one hundred "I'm sorrys," why don't you just
change?
Time will slow down so moments can be captured to open our
eyes to protect us from the wickedness
amongst us that lies.

Inspired by deceit and manipulation.

Dedicated to Andre M. (From D.C.)

Questions

How did I end up in the penitentiary?
when I was a perfect student in elementary?
How did a childhood end up sour?
Why am I down twenty-three and up one hour?
How can a man be so cold, or?
a woman allows her body to be sold.
Why did things happen that can't be told?
When will things ever change?
Why do things seem to stay the same?
Even after we constantly change lanes.
Why do questions go unanswered, or answers are given
to questions not asked?
Why does race matter when our blood is the same color?
Why don't I love them the same as the ones birthed by
my mother?
They're my father's children, so they're still my sisters
and brothers.
Why does being in love make you feel high or when the
heart's broken, it feels as if you'll die?
Why won't they listen for one minute to what I've got to
say, but they'll read what I write all day?

Inspired by questions I can't answer. June 6th, 2011.

It's Been Written

Tomorrow is here as yesterday is done.
Yesterday was once today as today has just begun.
We dream to strive, and we strive to accomplish.
We accomplish to succeed.
So now I'm accomplished waiting on success.
What will be done is set to come.
We believe in what's not seen,
knowing in faith it will come to pass.
What hurt will heal, what you can't touch you soon will
feel. The deepest will becomes shallow.
If you knew or if you didn't all what is to be, it's been
written.

Inspired by people who don't believe in dreams and all
that I do, now and forever. June 14th, 2011.

My Fire

My fire takes me places like smoke traveling through
Chicago, or like the strength slaves had five hundred
years ago.
Along the way we got weak, yet now each day we grow.
Soon our wisdom will show.
We'll do what we do; still, we'll know.
The flesh will heal like butter to a burn.
To make mistakes we'll all have our turn.
But it's not about the mistakes, yet the lessons we learn.
There's so much within I admire
but there's nothing like my fire.

Inspired by my strengths, determination, ambition, and
vision. 2011.

I Didn't Die

As I get older,
I try not to let prison make my heart grow colder,
I'm just a man with the world on his shoulders.
I wonder who misses me.
I miss a lot, but most of all I miss being free.
We learn in life things aren't always what they seem to
be. Sometimes we win, sometimes we lose.
We'll heal after we bruise.
We've just got to fight and understand we can't lose
sight. One day this darkness will be captured by a light
that shines bright.
Sometimes I cry and my daughter is so curious,
she asks why?
A lot of y'all left and didn't even say goodbye.
And it's like I couldn't get it right no matter how hard I try.
I'm just in prison…I didn't die.

Inspired by being eleven days away from 26 years old.

Dedicated to all those who showed up to my sentencing
yet haven't written me one letter. September 1st, 2011.

Understand Me

You may love me, or you may hate me.
I may have hurt you or you may have hurt me.
Let us sit down in a quiet room and listen to our body languages.
You may ask why I can't be still.
I'll watch the way you stand, without making a sound.
I'll bite my nails wherever I go.
But if you know me, this you'll know.
I've cried, I've screamed, I've even fallen on the ground, all due to a broken heart.
But that's another part.
Okay, are you ready?
Now start. Do you get what I want you to see?
Please just observe and understand me?

Inspire by being misunderstood and lack of an understanding.

Dedicated to those who observe. September 22nd, 2011.

<u>Written With Tears</u>

In this cell alone I lay, while my mind wanders away.
Trying to explain to my youngest daughter why I can't
come over and play.
Born three days after I was indicted,
to see her born I was so excited.
Now I can't give up, so I continue to fight it.
All that keeps me imprisoned, not just my flesh alone.
Constantly reminded of where I went wrong.
As I listen to the steel door close behind me,
enduring things they'll never see.
Hurting deep inside.
Learned only in the shower, my tears I can hide.
I look around wondering where's everyone who said
they'd always be by my side.
Some looked the other way, while some tried.
The strange things are some acts as if I died.
So, I share with all my peers, all that's written with tears.

Inspired by being isolated, alone, writing in tears for
someone to listen and care.

Dedicated to those whom I reached out to. September
22nd, 2011.

Cry

We cry when we hurt, we cry when we feel good.
We cry while asking why.
We cry about how hard we try.
Tears fall before and after a deep sigh.
Pain ignites our tears.
Tears flow when we experience our deepest fears.
When welcomed back, or when we say our final
goodbyes. We can't hold back the tears from our eyes.
So, however you feel let go and just cry.

Inspired by so many tears. December 11th, 2017.

Because of You

Because of you Lord, I can stand tall.
Because of you I get up every time I fall.
Because of you Lord all my pain is gone.
Because of you I wrote this poem.
I remember when I couldn't breathe,
and I fell down on my knees.
Felt as though I was choking,
because my heart and my spirit were broken.
My mother and father forsaken me.
I ended up so many places I didn't want to be.
Blinded by a cruel world I couldn't see.
I was in prison, but now I'm free,
I was broken but now I'm healed.
And God knows how I feel.
I felt I was all alone,
in the creator is where I found my home.
I didn't fit in with the world because I didn't belong.
Many nights I've cried until God came by my side,
To get it right Lord knows I tried.
Because of you Lord I can stand tall.
Because of you I get up every time I fall.
Because of you Lord all my pain is gone.
Because of you I wrote this poem.
When my childhood went astray,
and I didn't know how to pray.
I was just a boy; I didn't know what to say.
But even then, you paved the way.
You gave me all the love I was lacking,
because they all went on as if nothing happened.
And now I stand, tall, cause you show up every time
I call. They said I wouldn't make it.
I was just a child back then I couldn't take it.
Age fourteen I was on my own,
I wasn't welcomed in my momma home.
Been in prison for so long.
I remember not getting any mail,

felt like I was going through hell.
But you showed me it was me whom you adore.
Told me to hold on, and when I'm weak you'll be strong.
Told me to run the race,
and even just the size of a mustard seed to have faith.
Because of you Lord, I can stand tall Because of you
I get up every time I fall.
Because of you Lord all my pain is gone.
Because of you I wrote this poem.
You took away the pain,
released me of all of those chains.
Because of you I'm not the same.
I thank you Lord for saving my life.
You are the way, the Truth, and the Light.
Now I'm a new creature who fight.
I love you with all my heart,
You loved me from the very start.
Because of my sins I was lost,
you paid with your blood the ultimate cost.
So, I bow in worship before you on the cross.
You know the beginning and the end to my story.
That's why I praise you and give you all of the glory.
You took me out of a dark place,
 You are the author and finisher of my faith.
Now I'm not worrying nor stressing,
I'm thanking you Lord and counting all my blessings.
Because of you Lord, I can stand tall.
Because of you I get up every time I fall.
Because of you Lord all my pain is gone.
Because of you I wrote this poem.

Inspired by believing in a God that's real.

Dedicated to everyone who struggle with faith just hold
on. November 2016.

If I Die Before I wake

If I die before I wake, I pray the Lord my soul to take.
Forgive my sins in Jesus' sake.
To my mother, pursue what your heart desires.
Continue to smile and know in your heart God has your child.
To my father, to me your absence wasn't logical.
Still, you're my father, at least biological.
Auntie Pookie, now you're the best,
and I hope one day you put down them cigarettes.
Also live life with no regrets.
Shaad, you hold so much inside, let it go.
I know you smile to hide, so that the pain won't show.
Shea, I love you in a unique way.
I'm sorry I left home; please understand why in his home
I couldn't stay.
Baby Artis, I was the first born and you were the last.
Know in life there will be some tests you won't pass.
Julicia you're my first born.
You shared with me a secret I've never forgot.
Remember to strive hard to give it all you've got.
Ju, my boy, you're my only son.
I know in life you'll have your fun.
When it comes to responsibilities certain things have to be
done. Remember all the things I've said,
 even read a few of the books I've read.
Ju'Niyah, my last-born baby girl,
understand that your education will be your credentials.
Release all within to use your full potential.
When you all think of me smile at the moon.
Don't cry because I died too soon.
To all of you, my soul is at rest.
No more with myself do I have to fight.
Through it all try hard to understand what I write.
As far as the world, well that's a different note.
All those who never knew me,
you'll find pieces of myself in the things I've wrote.

Inspire by love, pain, and all the those who I'll leave behind
that I love. May 7th, 2011.

Chapter 8: My Pen & Me

"Delight yourself also in the Lord, and He shall give you the desires of your heart."

-Psalm 37:4

Breathe-Write

Breathe-write, breathe-write.
To stop writing is like holding my breath or to give me death.
Breathe-write, breathe-write.
It gives me good health. The pen is my heartbeat, the paper is my body, and the words are my blood flow, the sentences are my touch, my thoughts, and my sight.
Breathe-write, breathe-write.
I can feel my heart beating, pounding through my body I can feel my blood flow, I can touch you. I share my thoughts and my sight; now you can see what I see.
Breathe-write, breathe-write.
If I continue to breathe and write,
I'll continue to live and write what breath gives.

Inspired by living. December 28th, 2008.

With This Pen

Chop my hand off, I'm still going to write.
Even if you don't think I'm right or if I write things you
dislike. With this pen I can win any fight.
Bring sun rays that'll shine bright, in the midst of any
night. With this pen, I'll be around a hundred more years,
to settle their fears and dry all their tears.
With this pen, I can touch souls no matter how young or
old. Man, woman, boy or girl.
I'm talking the entire world.
With this pen, I can teach, I can preach, I can seek, I can
greet, and all I need is one pen and one sheet.
With this pen, I can make war without a sound.
I can paint a picture that can't be drew.
I can show people things they've never knew.
I can show you from the first time I picked this pen up till
now how much I've grew.
With this pen, I can take you places you've never been.
Just know the things that could be created and
destroyed,
lost and found, remembered, and forgotten, all with this
pen.

Inspired by my pen and our relationship. June 09, 2009.

I'm a Writer

I'm so much, while it all makes me a Writer.
I could bring fire with this pen like a match or a lighter.
I'm humble like a pit bull that's not a biter.
I'm a warrior like a Zulu tribe fighter.
I sustain in the darkness because it will soon get brighter.
When I find myself at a disadvantage I buckle down
tighter. Who knows what tomorrow will bring?
With this pen I'm great like an ancient African King.
If I obtain it, I don't worry about a thing.
It's my sword; I am so brave.
Without it I'm lost like a runaway slave.
At sea, on foreign land, so I write as much as I can.
So, you could all understand me, not only as a writer,
but also, as a man.
I'm so much, while it all makes me a writer.

Inspired by being and realizing that I'm a writer. Just
29th, 2009.

The Cage Bird that Wrote

Destined to fly, although he's held down,
he'll continue to try. Time is life, so he writes to get by.
Can feel the breeze so, he waits patiently to feel it
through his wings.
For the time being, he writes about so many things.
Contemplating, deep in thought, about what freedom
brings. Knowing within it's not as far as it seems.
The sun will shine forever, despite the worst weather.
It's nature's way of telling us things will always get better.
As the clouds shed countless tears,
and the sun gently wipes them away,
many won't hear what he had to say.
But if just someone receives this note,
 the entire world will hear about the caged bird that wrote.

Inspired by writing to the world while trapped in a cage.
June 12th, 2011.

Dedicated to Maya Angelou.

I Just Write

Just writing because people say I can write.
But those who can fight, don't just fight,
because they can fight.
I guess being a fighter is so much different than being a
writer. People say, "You're a poet," but those are just my
thoughts and feelings, I just write to show it.
So, I write, I write in the daytime, I write at nighttime.
I even write while doing hard time.
While crying, I write about love, hate, living, and dying.
I think I'd write even if I were blind.
So, I just write, and the more I write,
I realize people are right.

Inspired by thoughts and just wanting to write. June 11th,
2008.

I'd Rather be a Writer

My brother says I should be a rapper because my words rhyme. I told him I only rhyme some of the time.
Plus, I'd rather be a writer and leave souls burning like an out-of-control forest fire.
 My other brother says I should be a lawyer because my words are very convincing. But I'd rather be a writer, and let my words be influencing.
My mother says I should be an artist and paint pictures. In fact, I do. I'd rather be a writer and paint pictures that can't be drew.
When I was young, my stepfather told me I'd be just like my father.
I didn't know exactly what my father was like; but I know that I just wanted to write.
With all the suggestions and criticism, it is one thing I do know: I'd rather be a writer.

Inspired by thoughts, experiences and wanting to be a writer. July 11th, 2008.

What I Write

What I Write…
I want it to create sight, like a candle in the midst of the night.

What I Write…
I want it to stick to you for a while, like a spider bite.

What I Write…
can't change the world; but it just might.

What I Write…
is like the sun that shines so bright.

What I Write…
can hold you together like a thousand ropes tied tight.

What I Write…
will soar high in the sky like a kite.

What I Write…
will run deep like oil pipes.

What I Write…
will bring us together and for a noble cause we'll fight.
I am what I write…

Inspired by writing, July 13th, 2008.

What I Write Now

Metaphorically speaking,
my thoughts drip on paper like a water faucet that's
leaking.
It will be a part of you forever,
like a disease that makes you change your soul.
Not something curable like a common cold.
It'll be the story that must be told,
or as a jewel that's priceless and can't be sold.
When you get it you'll know for a fact.
It'll go recorded like history in an almanac.
It'll stick with you like a thumb tack.
It will guide you at dusk 'til dawn,
prepare you for the front line as if you were a pawn.
Some will be grandiose as well as discreet.
Still, my writings I want you to seek.
To understand why and how the things I go through,
have brought me to write about what I write now.

Inspired by writing. May 7th, 2011.

What I Continue to Write

What I write is louder than words spoken.
What I write is deeper than the deepest ocean.
What I write puts pictures in motion.
What I write is smooth, like a mixture of baby oil and lotion.
What I write can give the lame strength to walk.
What I write will make the deaf hear and the mute talk.
What I write will even give the blind sight.
What I write will change the world overnight.
What I write, we don't need a war to understand; we don't have to fight.
What I write, I want you to please listen.
What I write will give you all the things you're missing.
What I write could hold us together like water in a dam.
What I write altogether is who I am.

Inspired by what I write, May 7th, 2011.

<u>Before I'm Told I Can't Write</u>

Glue my pen in my hand,
just make sure that it doesn't run out of ink.
when you finish reading, breathe, then blink.
I know it'll blow your mind how I feel and what I think.
I'll write forever and eventually I'll get much better.
What I write is the cure to all the pain we endure.
Through writing, it allows me to be pure.
I'll write until it's over, that's for sure.
So, when you read what I write,
whether it's about the dark or light.
Listen to my tears and smile when I overcome my fears.
Honestly, I'd rather lose my sight before I'm told I can't
write.

Inspired by loving to write. June 10th, 2011.

<u>More Than Just Writing</u>

A fighter like penicillin, conscious.
So, I make my own decisions.
I was just an adolescent when I had a vision.
To write, to make them listen
because the lack of understanding is what they're
missing.
Allow me to tell the truth for a second.
We all want to grasp hold of life's lessons.
Although all will be tested.
We'll ask questions that go unanswered.
Like, "Where is God when a seven-year-old is being
molested?"
Somethings will try our faith.
But giving up can never be the case,
Because at times we feel we can't go on,
He'll be there in place.
Thank God for today because it's worth two tomorrows,
and so much more than yesterday.
Yesterday's pain is today's strength and today's strength
is tomorrow's success.
So don't speak on it; just allow your actions to confess.
It'll be seen in the dark like bright lightning.
So, understand, I'm doing more than just writing.

Inspired by believing in what I write. September 30th,
2011.

<u>OUTRODUCTION</u>

I write to get out the streets. I just want more out of life than me going to a funeral every weekend or running red lights because I'm worried about getting shot up. August 21, 2020 I was shot multiple times by a family member while sitting in the car.

R.I.P.

NICO

VONTE

MONSTA

T-MONEY

Made in the USA
Middletown, DE
25 January 2022